WHAT A YEAR IT WAS!

19 46

A walk back in time...

To

From

Media

Dedicated to America's World War II veterans,
with gratitude for their sacrifices.

Publishers • Lawrence Siegel & Art Worthington
Writing & Research • Beverly Cohn
Graphics • Peter Hess & Marguerite Jones

www.FLICKBACK.com
(800) 541-3533

Contents

Arts
&
Entertainment

Columbia Pictures announces **Rita Hayworth**'s *wardrobe for* Gilda *will cost a small fortune—$60,000.*

Movies

The Master Hits the Mark

Hot on the heels of last year's high-grossing hit, *Spellbound*, director **Alfred Hitchcock** strikes another box-office bullseye with the thrilling romance *Notorious*. Both films feature the luminous **Ingrid Bergman**, but are disimilar in many ways. While the pseudo-psychological *Spellbound* finds **Gregory Peck** earnestly plumbing his inner depths to vanquish the homicidal demons which haunt him, *Notorious* has suave **Cary Grant** at the heart of a sophisticated espionage caper. In addition to a torrid, record-breaking three-minute kiss between the leads, *Notorious* features that edge-of-the-seat tension which built the reputation of the "Master of Suspense." *Notorious* will come to be regarded as quintessential Hitchcock—one of the greatest of his career.

What's Playing AT THE MOVIES

GREAT EXPECTATIONS
GREEN FOR DANGER
THE HARVEY GIRLS
It's A Wonderful Life
THE JOLSON STORY
THE KILLERS
THE LOST WEEKEND
The Macomber Affair
My Darling Clementine
NOTORIOUS
Odd Man Out
OPEN CITY
The Postman Always Rings Twice
THE RAZOR'S EDGE
Song of the South
The Spiral Staircase
Stairway to Heaven
Three Little Girls in Blue
Three Strangers
THE YEARLING
Ziegfeld Follies

Anna and the King of Siam
Beauty and the Beast
The Best Years of Our Lives
THE BIG SLEEP
THE BLUE DAHLIA
BLUE SKIES
Brief Encounter
DECEPTION
DUEL IN THE SUN
Gilda

"I had to have her love even if I hung for it!"

M-G-M presents one of the year's outstanding films, based on James M. Cain's daring novel...

LANA **TURNER** · JOHN **GARFIELD** in
The Postman Always Rings Twice

with
Cecil Kellaway · Hume Cronyn · Leon Ames · Audrey Totter · Alan Reed
Screen Play by Harry Ruskin and Niven Busch · Based on the Novel by James Cain
Directed by TAY GARNETT · Produced by CAREY WILSON
A Metro-Goldwyn-Mayer Picture

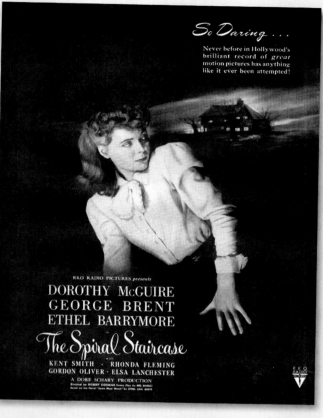

So Daring...
Never before in Hollywood's brilliant record of *great* motion pictures has anything like it ever been attempted!

RKO RADIO PICTURES presents

DOROTHY **McGUIRE**
GEORGE **BRENT**
ETHEL **BARRYMORE**
in
The Spiral Staircase

with
KENT SMITH · RHONDA FLEMING
GORDON OLIVER · ELSA LANCHESTER

A DORE SCHARY PRODUCTION
Directed by ROBERT SIODMAK · Screen Play by MEL DINELLI
Based on the Novel "Some Must Watch" by ETHEL LINA WHITE

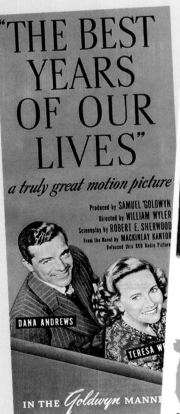

"THE BEST YEARS OF OUR LIVES"

a truly great motion picture

Produced by SAMUEL GOLDWYN
Directed by WILLIAM WYLER
Screenplay by ROBERT E. SHERWOOD
From the Novel by MACKINLAY KANTOR
Released thru RKO Radio Pictures

DANA ANDREWS

TERESA W...

IN THE *Goldwyn* MANNE...

DAVID O. SELZNICK presents

COMING THIS FALL

GREGORY **PECK**

JENNIFER **JONES**

JOSEPH **COTTEN**

with
LIONEL BARRYMORE · HERBERT MARSHALL
LILLIAN GISH · WALTER HUSTON
CHARLES BICKFORD

DUEL in the SUN
IN TECHNICOLOR

PARAMOUNT FOUND THE COURAGE AND DARING TO FILM THIS STRANGE, POWERFUL AND TERRIFYING NOVEL. THROUGH SKILL AND GREAT PERFORMANCES IT EMERGES AS ONE OF THE MOST REMARKABLY THRILLING ACHIEVEMENTS IN MOTION PICTURE ENTERTAINMENT.

"The Lost Weekend"

Ray Milland and Jane Wyman in "The Lost Weekend". From the Novel by Charles Jackson with Phillip Terry, Howard da Silva, Doris Dowling, Frank Faylen · Produced by Charles Brackett · Directed by Billy Wilder · Screen Play by Charles Brackett and Billy Wilder

Oscar® Night in Hollywood

With the public mood lightening following the end of World War II, glamour returns at the 18th Annual Academy Awards ceremony. Bob Hope and James Stewart host the evening at Graumann's Chinese Theatre in Hollywood.

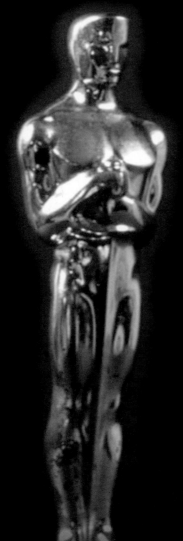

Among the film notables attending this gala evening are:

Myrna Loy and Gene Markey *(top)*

Margaret O'Brien *(right)* and

Ann Blyth and mom *(below).*

Ann Revere
receives her Oscar for Best
Supporting Actress in
National Velvet.

Ingrid Bergman presents Ray Milland with the
Best Actor award for his dramatic starring role
in the harrowing film, *The Lost Weekend.*

★

Billy Wilder *(left)* and Charles
Brackett are honored for their
Lost Weekend Best Screenplay.

Jean Hersholt, representing the
Board of Governors, presents
Bob Hope with a mini-mini-
mini version of the coveted
Oscar as their way of saying
"thank you" for acting as
master of ceremonies for the
last seven years.

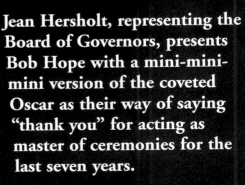

The Academy Awards

"And The Winner Is..."

Oscars® Presented in 1946

BEST PICTURE
THE LOST WEEKEND

BEST ACTOR
RAY MILLAND, *The Lost Weekend*

BEST ACTRESS
JOAN CRAWFORD, *Mildred Pierce*

BEST DIRECTOR
BILLY WILDER, *The Lost Weekend*

BEST SUPPORTING ACTOR
JAMES DUNN, *A Tree Grows in Brooklyn*

BEST SUPPORTING ACTRESS
ANNE REVERE, *National Velvet*

BEST SONG
"It Might As Well Be Spring"

Joan Crawford

1946 Favorites (Oscars® Presented in 1947)

BEST PICTURE
THE BEST YEARS OF OUR LIVES

BEST ACTOR
FREDRIC MARCH, *The Best Years of Our Lives*

BEST ACTRESS
OLIVIA DE HAVILLAND, *To Each His Own*

BEST DIRECTOR
WILLIAM WYLER, *The Best Years of Our Lives*

BEST SUPPORTING ACTOR
HAROLD RUSSELL, *The Best Years of Our Lives*

BEST SUPPORTING ACTRESS
ANNE BAXTER, *The Razor's Edge*

BEST SONG
"On The Atchison, Topeka And Santa Fe"

Fredric March

12

Hollywood

Types it's Beauties

Marie McDonald
"The Body"

Lizabeth Scott
Cafe-Society

Lana Turner
Glamorous

Hedy Lamarr
Classical European

Maureen O'Hara
Romantic

Despite her position as a Star, **Ginger Rogers**, *unlike most other Stars, prefers to do her own movie screaming rather than using a professional screamer.*

WONDERFUL! WONDERFUL! WONDERFUL!

HOW COULD IT BE ANYTHING ELSE?

LIBERTY FILMS, INC. presents

FRANK CAPRA'S
WONDERFILM
"IT'S A WONDERFUL LIFE"
starring
JAMES STEWART
and DONNA REED
...as Jimmy's girl!

Tops even Capra's three Academy Award winners: "It Happened One Night" "Mr. Deeds Goes to Town" and "You Can't Take It With You!"

He couldn't do anything right!

He couldn't do anything wrong!

He couldn't do *anything!*

with LIONEL BARRYMORE • THOMAS MITCHELL • HENRY TRAVERS • Beulah Bondi • Ward Bond • Frank Faylen
Gloria Grahame • Produced and Directed by FRANK CAPRA • Screenplay by Frances Goodrich • Albert Hackett and Frank Capra • Additional Scenes by Jo Swerling • From a story by Philip Van Doren Stern • Released through RKO Radio Pictures

14

Arts & Entertainment

★ BORN *in* 1946 ★

BLAIR BROWN
SALLY FIELD
TOMMY LEE JONES
DIANE KEATON
DAVID LYNCH
SUSAN SARANDON
TALIA SHIRE
GENE SISKEL
CARRIE SNODGRESS
STEVEN SPIELBERG
SYLVESTER STALLONE
OLIVER STONE

Sally Field

Walt Disney's *SONG OF THE SOUTH* is one of the earliest feature films to combine live action footage with animation and is the first Disney feature in which live actors are hired for lead roles.

France holds it's first CANNES FILM FESTIVAL.

After years of tangling with censors, **Howard Hughes**' steamy western *THE OUTLAW* starring bosomy **Jane Russell** is released in a newly-edited version. Despite the cuts, a San Francisco theater owner is arrested for showing a film "offensive to decency."

HOLLYWOOD BIDS A FOND FAREWELL

Versatile character actor **NOAH BEERY** (64) specialized in playing heavies and villains in the silent film era and in early talkies. His brother, Wallace Beery, was a well-known actor as was his son, Noah Beery, Jr.

W.C. FIELDS (66), one of the screen's most successful comic actors, dies on Christmas. Born William Claude Dunkenfield to vegetable-selling parents in Philadelphia, Fields developed juggling and pool-playing skills at a young age before becoming an entertainer and appearing in musical theatre and the Ziegfeld Follies. His first film role came in 1915 and thereafter he settled in Burbank, California, making dozens of movies for Paramount. Among his most famous: *Never Give a Sucker An Even Break* (1941), *The Bank Dick* (1940), and *My Little Chickadee* (1940).

William S. Hart

"Two-gun Bill" **WILLIAM S. HART** (82) was the original movie cowboy. A successful Broadway stage actor, he made his first film, a 2-reeler, in 1914 and his final, *Tumbleweeds*, in 1925 for United Artists. He retired to his ranch in Newhall near Los Angeles, which he deeded to the city for use as a park.

W.C. Fields with Mae West in My Little Chickadee.

15

Television

O nly the DuMont Network and NBC program evening broadcasts in the U.S. On Sunday night, DuMont viewers see a Western film for an hour, another hour on Tuesday, and half-hours on Wednesday and Thursday nights. NBC offers an hour of programs on Sunday, two hours on Thursday, and the *Gillette Cavalcade of Sports* on Monday and Friday nights.

On The BBC

BRITISH BROADCASTING CORPORATION

The BBC resumes postwar broadcasting on June 7th, beginning with the same **Mickey Mouse** cartoon—**Mickey's Gala Premiere**—that had been the last program transmitted seven years earlier at the outbreak of World War II. The cartoon is preceded by the announcement: "As we were saying before we were so rudely interrupted..."

One of the few pre-war programs to return to the BBC is kids' show **For The Children**.

Telecrime, the first television crime series from the 1930s, also returns with the new title, **Telecrimes**.

The Children's puppet show Muffin the Mule *debuts, featuring Annette Mills, sister of actor John Mills.*

The first televised heavyweight boxing title fight is broadcast from Yankee Stadium on June 19th. 141,000 people watch **Joe Louis**— fresh from a 4-year army stint—KO an overmatched **Billy Conn** in the eighth round of what some consider a disappointing match.

RCA demonstrates an all-electronic color television system.

Tokyo Tushin Kogyo is founded, later to become SONY.

ZOOMAR introduces the first professional zoom lens.

The first television network soap opera, *Faraway Hill,* airs on the DUMONT NETWORK.

The first church service is telecast from Grace Episcopal Church in New York.

Be FIRST in TELEVISION with VIEWTONE!

Approximately $100

First

...with low-cost television. Receivers priced at approximately $100—Television for everyone!

First

...with its offer to dealers of a well balanced line of radios, combinations, record players and television sets embodying postwar engineering marvels, brilliant new design, cabinet beauty, amazing tone, and sensational price structure.

First

..with the announcement to the public of definite plans for production of television receivers for the mass market, incorporating all advance features possible at low cost—as well as the full story on the rest of the line.

First

..with a public "mass demonstration" of its entire line, including "$100" television.

The photograph shows a small part of the enthusiastic audience of over 6000 people who saw a performance demonstration of VIEWTONE LOW COST PRACTICAL TELEVISION in a New York department store. Public acceptance was terrific. People wanted to buy right then and there. VIEWTONE TELEVISION proved itself at its first presentation to the public.

Get your share of immediate sales—big profits from the Viewtone line. America's most talked about Television and Radio Sets

WRITE FOR THE FACTS TODAY

VIEWTONE COMPANY

Office: 203 E. 18th St., New York 3, N.Y. • Factory Site: B'klyn, N.Y.

Dr. Peter C. Goldmark, 39-year old inventor of color television, introduces post-war equipment that produces vivid colors prompting CBS to announce the seemingly unsolvable problems had been solved and that if the demand is there, color television could be enjoyed in American homes within a year.

American Federation of Musicians bars its members from television performances pending investigation into the impact on the radio industry.

Construction Of Television Transmitter Completed On Mt. Wilson, California Extends Reception Radius To 100 Miles – Three Times The Radius Of A Lowland Station.

CBS
Builds New Television Receiver Compatible With Black And White And Color Transmissions.

★ BORN *in* 1946 ★

LONI ANDERSON
CANDICE BERGEN
BARRY BOSTWICK
CONNIE CHUNG
PATTY DUKE
MARY BETH HURT
CRAIG T. NELSON
PRISCILLA PRESLEY
SUSAN ST. JAMES
LESLEY ANN WARREN

Connie Chung

Radio

TOP 10 *Daytime Radio Shows*

1. When A Gal Marries
2. Young Widder Brown
3. Our Gal Sunday
4. Portia Faces Life
5. Kate Smith Speaks
6. Ma Perkins
7. Breakfast In Hollywood
8. Aunt Jenny
9. Right To Happiness
10. Romance Of Helen Trent

TOP 10 *Evening Radio Shows*

1. Jack Benny
2. Fibber McGee & Molly
3. Bob Hope
4. Charlie McCarthy Show
5. Fred Allen
6. Radio Theatre
7. Amos 'n' Andy
8. Walter Winchell
9. Red Skelton
10. Screen Guild Players

Jack Benny, left, and Fred Allen

BING CROSBY is riding high as his movie, *The Bells of St. Mary's*, is one of the year's top grossers, *The Road to Rio* and *The Road to Utopia*—the 4th and 5th of his popular "buddy" pictures with pal **BOB HOPE**—await release, his records are perennial chart-toppers, and he inks a radio contract paying him a record $30,000 weekly.

Bing Crosby and Bob Hope

Cass Daley Becomes Radio's Most Popular Comedienne.

Superman Battles Intolerance

On the popular *Adventures of Superman* radio program, the Man of Steel tackles a new enemy: bigotry. "Remember this as long as you live," he tells his young listeners, "Whenever you meet up with anyone who is trying to cause trouble between people—anyone who tries to tell you that a man can't be a good citizen because of his religious beliefs—you can be sure that troublemaker is a rotten citzen himself and an inhuman being. Don't ever forget that!"

Massive panic, including suicides, results from a French National Radio broadcast of tongue-in-cheek bulletins announcing accidental atomic explosions which are shattering cities and destroying the world.

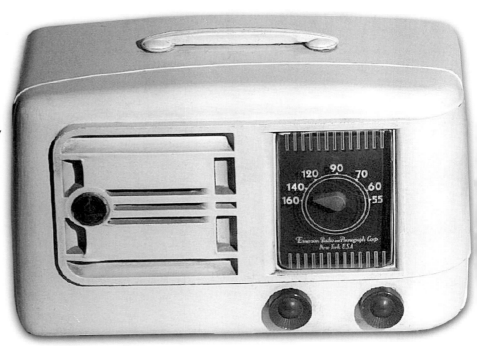

- Proponents of FM radio charge that AM network and independent stations are trying to hamstring the progress of FM accessibility which many agree will occupy a major place in the future of radio.

- **Abe Burrows**, called the greatest living satirist by the late **Robert Benchley**, begins writing a new CBS comedy show called *Holiday & Co.* for a salary of $3,000 weekly.

- Removal of wartime restrictions unleashes unprecedented demand for new or augmented radio services.

- **Frank Stanton** is elected president of CBS.

Virginia Payne, radio's Ma Perkins.

- CBS announces one of the first and biggest buyers of soap-opera time, PROCTER & GAMBLE, renewed four long-running Programs—**Ma Perkins, Road Of Life, Life Can Be Beautiful** and **Young Dr. Malone** for another season.

- ZENITH RADIO and its president, Commander **Eugene F. McDonald**, Jr., support WWZR-FM in Chicago to the tune of $75,000 yearly to offer radio listeners a commercial-free, music-only alternative to the roar of commercial radio.

65,000 Hats Are Entered In Hedda Hopper's Hat Contest.

24

POPULAR MUSIC

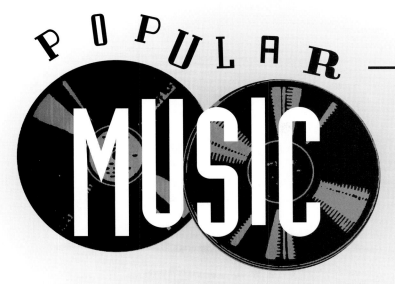

THE YEAR'S BIG RECORDS

Choo Choo Ch' Boogie **Louis Jordan**
Doin' What Comes Natur'lly **Dinah Shore**
I'm Always Chasing Rainbows **Perry Como**
The Old Lamplighter **Kay Kyser**
Shoo Fly Pie and Apple Pan Dowdy
Stan Kenton w/**June Christy**
They Say It's Wonderful **Frank Sinatra**

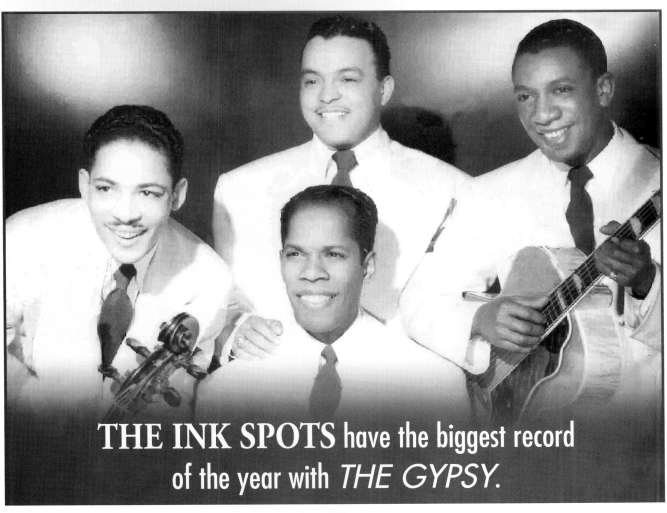

THE INK SPOTS have the biggest record
of the year with *THE GYPSY.*

NEW ALBUMS

DECCA

MANUFACTURED BY DECCA RECORDS, INC., NEW YORK, U.S.A

DECCA RECORDING STARS

ANDREWS SISTERS

CARMEN CAVALLARO

KENNY BAKER

BING CROSBY

CHARLIE BARNET

JIMMY DORSEY

CONNIE BOSWELL

JIMMY DURANTE

KITTY CARLISLE

DEANNA DURBIN

PERCY FAITH

ELLA FITZGERALD

HELEN FORREST

JUDY GARLAND

GLENN GRAY

LIONEL HAMPTON

DICK HAYMES

HILDEGARDE

JIMMY LUNCEFORD

LOUIS JORDAN

INK SPOTS

GUY LOMBARDO

MARY MARTIN

MILLS BROTHERS

BURL IVES

FRED WARING

RUSS MORGAN

VICTOR YOUNG

ETHEL SMITH

The Famous Austrian Trapp Family Singers Give Annual Christmas Concert In New York's Town Hall.

Fans turn out in record numbers for **DUKE ELLINGTON'S** *Carnegie Hall Concert.*

Ellington

Woody Herman fan **Igor Stravinsky** writes 8-minute *Ebony Concerto* for Herman's band.

Herman

TECHNI**COLOR**
*cavalcade of glorious
entertainment!*

Thrill
to these
beloved
melodies!

CALIFORNIA, HERE
I COME

SWANEE

YOU MADE ME LOVE YOU

MAMMY

WAITING FOR THE
ROBERT E. LEE

APRIL SHOWERS

I WANT A GIRL

RAINBOW 'ROUND MY
SHOULDER

LIZA

ROCKABYE YOUR BABY

BY THE LIGHT OF THE
SILV'RY MOON

ABOUT A QUARTER
TO NINE

I'M SITTING ON TOP
OF THE WORLD

TOOT, TOOT,
TOOTSIE

COLUMBIA
PICTURES presents

The JOLSON STORY

WITH

LARRY PARKS · EVELYN KEYES

WILLIAM DEMAREST · BILL GOODWIN

Screenplay by Stephen Longstreet
Produced by SIDNEY SKOLSKY
Directed by ALFRED E. GREEN

THE MUSIC..
THE MAGIC..
THE TIMES
of
AMERICA'S
GREATEST
ENTERTAINER!

28

POPULAR SONG HITS

All Through The Day

It's A Good Day

Anything You Can Do

La Vie En Rose

Aren't You Glad You're You

Linda

Come Rain Or Come Shine

Let It Snow, Let It Snow, Let It Snow

Day By Day

Oh, What It Seemed To Be

There's No Business Like Show Business

Doctor, Lawyer, Indian Chief

Old Devil Moon

Five Minutes More

They Say It's Wonderful

(Get Your Kicks On) Route 66

Ole Buttermilk Sky

This Heart Of Mine

Golden Earrings

Personality

To Each His Own

How Are Things In Glocca Morra

Rumors Are Flying

I Can't Begin To Tell You

Shangri-La

When I'm Not Near The Girl I Love

I Don't Know Enough About You

Some Day You'll Want Me To Want You

South America, Take It Away

You Always Hurt The One You Love

I Got The Sun In The Morning

Surrender

You Make Me Feel So Young

If This Isn't Love

Tenderly

You're Nobody 'Til Somebody Loves You

I'm A Big Girl Now

The Christmas Song

It Might As Well Be Spring

The Girl That I Marry

Zip-A-Dee-Doo-Dah

29

AL JOLSON revitalizes his career by re-recording his previous hits for the soundtrack of the film, *The Jolson Story*, making him a popular star with the post-World War II generation.

New Artists Launch Their Musical Careers

Chet Atkins

Dean Martin

Bill Haley

B. B. King

Little Walter

Have Baton, Will Travel

Three Young Conductors – Leonard Bernstein, Bernard Herrmann And Robert Lawrence – Represent America Abroad.

Arturo Toscanini Conducts At La Scala And Eric Leinsdorf Tours Europe.

Toscanini

Salzburg Festival Reopens

Pablo Casals Refuses Recital Invitations In America And England Because Of Their Recognition Of Franco's Spain.

Charles Ives

Veteran American Composer, Charles E. Ives, Receives Long Overdue Recognition As A Unique Phenomenon In Musical History.

George Szell Replaces Eric Leinsdorf As Cleveland Orchestra Conductor At A Salary Of $30,000 Yearly – Highest Ever Paid For That Job.

Arturo Toscanini, 78, Celebrates The 50th Anniversary Of The Premiere Of Puccini's "La Boheme" By Conducting The First Two Acts Over NBC Radio In What Is Hailed As The Best Performance Of The Opera In America Since He Conducted It At The Met In 1910.

OPERA DEBUTS

Benjamin Britten's **"THE RAPE OF LUCRETIA"**

Gian Carlo Menotti, **"The Medium"**

BORIS BLACHER'S Chamber Opera **"Die Flut"**

Britten

Igor Stravinsky Premieres "Symphony In Three Movements" And Aaron Copland Introduces "Symphony No. 3."

BENJAMIN BRITTEN'S OPERA, "PETER GRIMES," MAKES ITS AMERICAN DEBUT AT THE BERKSHIRE MUSIC FESTIVAL WITH LEONARD BERNSTEIN CONDUCTING.

Stravinsky

OPERA DEBUTS

Madame Butterfly

is performed at the Met for the first time since Pearl Harbor with a record number of fans turned away at the box office.

Samuel Barber's "Concerto For Cello And Orchestra" Receives New York Music Critics Circle Award As The Best New American Work To Be Premiered In New York.

PULITZER PRIZE
LEO SOWERBY,
The Canticle Of The Sun

Ballets

Frederick Ashton's "Symphonic Variations"

BALANCHINE'S NIGHTSHADOW

Balanchine

Under The Choreographic Direction Of George Balanchine, The Ballet Russe de Monte Carlo Winds Up Its Longest Run Of Ballet In Manhattan History.

ON BROADWAY

Irving Berlin's musical comedy *Annie Get Your Gun* debuts with Ethel Merman in the starring role.

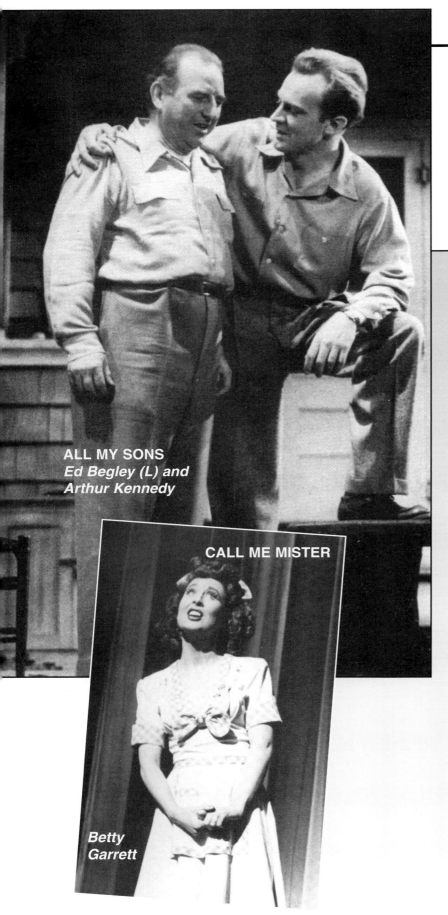

ALL MY SONS
*Ed Begley (L) and
Arthur Kennedy*

CALL ME MISTER

*Betty
Garrett*

PLAYS

All My Sons

Another Part Of
The Forest

Born Yesterday

Brigadoon

Call Me Mister

Joan Of Lorraine

Lute Song

St. Louis Woman

The Devil's General

The Iceman Cometh

The Winslow Boy

Pulitzer Prize

Russel Crouse & Howard Lindsay, "State Of The Union"

PASSINGS

Laurette Taylor, Stage Actress, Winner Of New York Drama Critics' Circle Award For Her Role As The Mother In "The Glass Menagerie," Dies At 62.

art

The U.S. War Department stores 200 masterpieces valued at $80,000,000 rescued from destroyed or damaged German museums until they are returned to Germany or their rightful owners.

Holland sends America a "Garland Of Thanks" by lending for exhibition 48 sixteenth- and seventeenth-century Dutch masterpieces looted by the Nazis.

new paintings

Fernand Leger
Composition With Branch

Marc Chagall
Cow With Umbrella

Graham Sutherland
Crucifixion

exhibitions

*Max Beckmann
self portrait*

German Expressionist **MAX BECKMANN**'s war works go on view in a Manhattan gallery for the first time.

GEORGIA O'KEEFFE is the first woman to exhibit at the Museum Of Modern Art.

HYMAN BLOOM, whose works appeared in the Museum of Modern Art's presentation, *Americans-1942*, holds his first one-man exhibition.

Georgia O'Keeffe

Young Sculptor **CHARLES SALERNO** debuts 14 works to critical acclaim.

Harvard's Fogg Museum mounts the most comprehensive Pre-Raphaelite show yet seen in the United States.

A major **GAUGUIN** show is mounted in a Manhattan gallery.

Gaugin

BILLY ROSE PAYS $75,000 FOR REMBRANDT'S "PILGRIM AT PRAYER" AT PARKE-BERNET AUCTION.

200 TOP U.S. ARTISTS REVEAL THEY EARN AN AVERAGE OF $1,154 A YEAR FROM THE SALE OF THEIR PAINTINGS.

Rembrandt self portrait

First Prize Winners In National Art Competitions

(A SAMPLING)

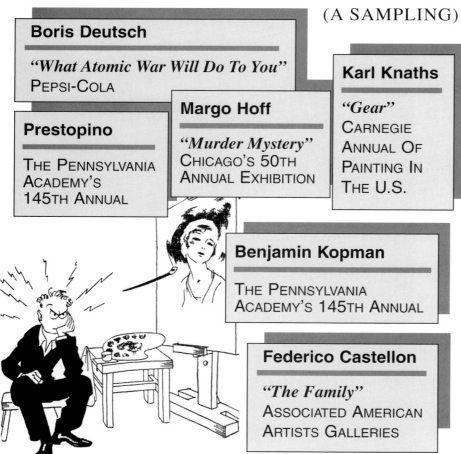

Boris Deutsch

"What Atomic War Will Do To You" PEPSI-COLA

Prestopino

THE PENNSYLVANIA ACADEMY'S 145TH ANNUAL

Margo Hoff

"Murder Mystery" CHICAGO'S 50TH ANNUAL EXHIBITION

Karl Knaths

"Gear" CARNEGIE ANNUAL OF PAINTING IN THE U.S.

Benjamin Kopman

THE PENNSYLVANIA ACADEMY'S 145TH ANNUAL

Federico Castellon

"The Family" ASSOCIATED AMERICAN ARTISTS GALLERIES

Francis Barone Wins $1,500 Fellowship In Pepsi Cola's Third Annual Competition For His Painting Entitled: "Lime Kiln."

Ralston Crawford, Well-Known Abstractionist, Is Selected As The Only Artist-Correspondent To Witness The Bikini Tests.

Photographer Alfred Stieglitz Dies At 82.

books

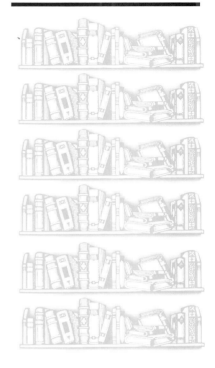

NOBEL PRIZE

LITERATURE

HERMANN HESSE
(Switzerland)

PULITZER PRIZE

HISTORY

ARTHUR M. SCHLESINGER, Jr.
The Age Of Jackson

BIOGRAPHY

LINNY MARSH WOLFE
Son Of The Wilderness

PASSINGS

GERTRUDE STEIN,
Author And Patron Of The Arts, Dies In France At 72.

H.G. WELLS,
Prolific Author Of Prophetic Science Fiction Books Including "The War Of The Worlds" And "The Time Machine" Dies At 79.

BOOTH TARKINGTON,
Two-Time Pulitzer Prize Winning Novelist And Playwright, Dies At 76.

DAMON RUNYON
Dies At 62.

books

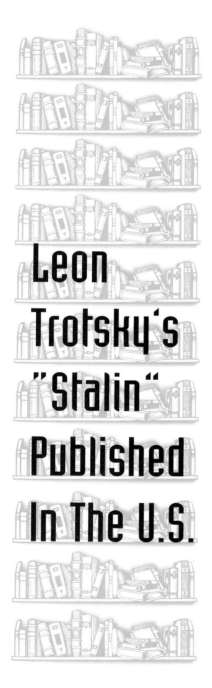

Leon Trotsky's "Stalin" Published In The U.S.

ALL THE KING'S MEN
Robert Penn Warren

ANIMAL FARM
George Orwell

ARC DE TRIOMPHE
E. M. Remarque

BABY AND CHILD CARE
Benjamin Spock

BACK
Henry Green

B. F.'S DAUGHTER
John P. Marquand

DEATH AND ENTRANCES
Dylan Thomas

DELTA WEDDING
Eudora Welty

HIROSHIMA
John Hersey

I THE JURY
Mickey Spillane

LADDERS TO FIRE
Anais Nin

MEMOIRS OF HECATE COUNTY
Edmund Wilson

MIRACLE DE LA ROSE
JEAN GENET

MR. BLANDINGS BUILDS HIS DREAM HOUSE
Eric Hodgins

RED ROSES FOR ME
Sean O'Casey

STALINGRAD
Theodore Plievier

THE ART OF PLAIN TALK
Rudolph Flesch

THE BERLIN STORIES
Christopher Isherwood

THE BIG CLOCK
Kenneth Fearing

THE CHRYSANTHEMUM AND THE SWORD
Ruth Benedict

THE FOXES OF HARROW
Frank Yerby

THE MEMBER OF THE WEDDING
Carson McCullers

THE PERENNIAL PHILOSOPHY
Aldous Huxley

THIS SIDE OF INNOCENCE
Taylor Caldwell

WILLOWAW
Gore Vidal

ZORBA THE GREEK
Nikos Kazantzakis

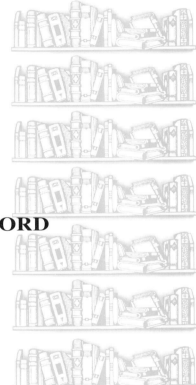

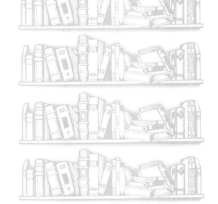

In The News

The Nuremberg Trials are underway at the Palace of Justice in Nuremberg, Germany. 22 Nazi officials are on trial for complicity in war crimes during World War II.

Prisoners are kept under close surveillance in their cells.

Sentenced to death by hanging, Luftwaffe Commander Hermann Göring commits suicide by cyanide in his cell before the sentence is enacted.

A prisoner's lunch.

United Nations Security Council Holds First Session in London

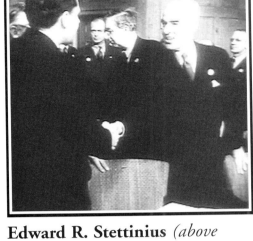

Edward R. Stettinius *(above right)*, United States delegate, shaking hands with British representative, **Ernest Bevin** attends this historic session.

Also in attendance for this important 11-member council is Russia's delegate, **Andrei Gromyko** *(right).*

■ U.N. Security Council condemns Spanish dictator **Franco**.

Franco

■ The League Of Nations is officially dissolved in a vote by 34 nations in Geneva.

■ First session of United Nations General Assembly held in London.

■ New York declared permanent home of the United Nations.

■ Site of the World's Fair in Flushing Meadows, New York designated as temporary home for the U.N. General Assembly.

■ **John D. Rockefeller, Jr.** donates $8.5 million toward new U.N. headquarters.

■ Statesman **Bernard Baruch** appointed U.S. representative to U.N. Atomic Energy Commission, calls for U.N. control of A-Bomb.

POLAND REBUILDS HER SHATTERED CITY

Warsaw, one of the first major European cities to fall under the Nazi blitz, embarks on rebuilding its capital.

After six years of war, some semblance of normal life begins to return to this war-torn city.

U.S. SUPREME COURT JUSTICES CALL FOR TOLERANCE

Supporting the American Brotherhood campaign, sponsored by the National Council of Christians and Jews, **Justice Frankfurter** states that:
"The unfolding of our Republic is the story of the greatest racial mixture in history. Of the 56 signers of the Declaration of Independence, 18 were of non-English stock... Foreign-born citizens of almost every land fought in the war for independence, helped save the union and in conspicuous numbers are found on the honor rolls of the two World Wars."

Chief **Justice Harlan Stone** in his plea for tolerance adds:
"Freedom of the mind and the spirit has its practical aspects in everyday life. It includes the right of every man to live and work in peace, to earn and to save and to enjoy the fruits of his labor, so long as their enjoyment does no harm to his neighbor..."

NAZI WAR CRIMINALS SENTENCED AT NUREMBERG TRIALS

Death Sentence:	Bormann, Frank, Frick, Goering, Jodl, Kaltenbrunner, Keitel, Ribbentrop, Rosenberg, Sauckel, Seyss-Inquart, Streicher
Life Imprisonment:	Funk, Hess, Raeder
20 Years Imprisonment:	Schirach, Speer
15 Years Imprisonment:	Neurath
10 Years Imprisonment:	Doenitz
Acquittals:	Fritsche, Schacht, von Papen

Attempts to revive the Nazi Party crushed by Allies who seize 1,000 Sympathizers. • Argentina provides safe haven for Nazis.

AMERICA has THE WORLD'S BIGGEST BOMBER!

B-36
Photographed on recent test flight

THIS is the giant B-36—the biggest land-based bomber ever built.

Manned by a crew of 15 men, it is designed to carry 10,000 pounds of bombs 10,000 miles. Its top speed is more than 300 miles per hour. Operating from airports available to us, the B-36 could, *if this country were attacked*, drop bombs on any city in the world.

Just how big is "the world's biggest bomber"?

Imagine a tail fin that is almost as tall as the average 5-story apartment building! Fuel tanks so large that more than 2 railroad tank cars are needed to fill them! Six pusher-type engines with a total of 18,000 horsepower! A wingspread as great as that of two B-24 Liberator bombers, with 10 feet to spare!

Designed and built by Consolidated Vultee, in conjunction with the United States Army Air Forces, the mammoth B-36 is a mighty symbol of peace-loving America's determination to remain strong in the air—to preserve the peace through strength!

The awe-inspiring B-36—first of a fleet of such long-range bombers now under construction—is one of Consolidated Vultee's important contributions to this nation's protective strength in the air.

And THE WORLD'S MOST MODERN TWIN-ENGINE AIRLINER is on the way!

CONVAIR 240

America's leadership in commercial aviation is a *must*, too.

Consolidated Vultee is now building the most modern twin-engine airliner the world has ever seen. This new transport, known as the Convair-240, will be flying the skyways next summer.

Many famous airlines—including American Airlines, Western Air Lines, Pan American World Airways, Continental Air Lines, and KLM (Royal Dutch Airlines) have already ordered fleets of Convair-240's.

Watch for this ultra-modern 300 MPH airliner—pressurized and air conditioned for your comfort.

We promise you that your first flight in the Convair-240 will be an experience you will want to repeat over and over again—whenever you want to travel *faster*, and with *greater safety* and *comfort!*

Let's keep America strong in the air!

Consolidated Vultee Aircraft Corporation

San Diego, California • Downey, California • Wayne, Michigan (Stinson Division) • Fort Worth, Texas • Nashville, Tennessee

53

At the request of President Truman, former president Herbert Hoover prepares to leave New York for Europe where his task is finding ways of averting starvation in nations torn by war.

Hoover In Italy

Mr. Hoover arrives in Rome and is greeted by Italian food minister de Gaspari.

In Italy, the work of the United Nations Relief Agency is already in effect as thousands of school children are fed daily under the supervision of the school authorities.

President Truman Approves Loan to Great Britain

President Truman calls the agreement: *"Good business for the industries of America, good business for our farmers, and good business for our workers... an important step in rebuilding foreign trade and in creating jobs in America. The alternative to the British loan is trade warfare between nations. Peace can be built only on a foundation of world economic cooperation and stability. The British loan is a cornerstone in the world's structure of peace."*

PRESIDENT TRUMAN CALLS FOR AMERICANS TO REDUCE FOOD CONSUMPTION TO HELP IN WORLD HUNGER FIGHT

EXCERPTS FROM SPEECH GIVEN APRIL 19, 1946.

"It is my duty to join my voice with the voices of humanity everywhere in behalf of the starving millions of human beings all over the world. We have a high responsibility, as Americans, to go to their rescue...

"We would not be Americans if we did not wish to share our comparative plenty with suffering people...

"America cannot remain healthy and happy in the same world where millions of human beings are starving...

"...we would all be better off physically and spiritually, if we ate less... Every slice of bread, every ounce of fat and oil saved by your voluntary sacrifice, will help keep starving people alive.

"By our combined effort, we will reduce starvation and with God's help, we will avert the worst of this plague of famine that follows in the wake of war. I ask every American now to pledge himself to share..."

President Truman creates Central Intelligence Group. • Chester Bowles heads newly created Office of Economic Stabilization. • W. Averell Harriman named U.S. Ambassador to Britain. • U.S. Supreme Court rules segregation in public transportation unconstitutional. • President Truman warns future atomic wars *"...May well destroy nations and change present standard of civilization."* • President Truman creates the Atomic Energy Commission. • Wisconsin elects Joe McCarthy to the Senate. • President Truman appoints Ambassador W. Averell Harriman Secretary of Commerce replacing Henry A. Wallace. • Republicans regain control of Congress. • Supreme Court grants Oregon Indians land payment rights from U.S. government. • December: President Truman formally ends World War II.

Ask him what oil he uses in his car!

(He's your independent dealer...with more than 800 brands to choose from)

1. "I use Macmillan" say 3 out of 5*. *"Why?* Just remember, all day long I'm looking under the hoods of different cars. I see proof that Macmillan oil removes hard carbon. Yes, and proof that this tough-film oil makes any car run smoother, longer!" Yes, any car...

2. Doc's car never gets sick! *His* expert prescribed good medicine for that '42 motor. "Macmillan oil," he said, "is right for hard, fast driving. Refined by an exclusive, patented process. Guards against heat and pressure." (No wonder this doctor wrote us a nice "thank you" note for helping to keep his car on the job. It's one of thousands in our files!)

3. "Miss Minnie, you need Macmillan! You're a quick-trip driver. Start-stop, start-stop. Why, your motor hardly ever gets warmed up. But Macmillan oil wiggles into the tightest spots—then clings and clings. It's *ready* when you step on the starter."

4. String along with your expert. Look for the Macmillan sign in your neighborhood. Drive in. Try a crankcase full of Macmillan Ring-Free. You'll find that it's *different*...there's no other oil in all the world just like it! *Cleans* as it *lubricates.*

Throughout the nation, *3 out of 5* **of these dealers* say —**

"I USE MACMILLAN IN MY CAR!"

Based on actual reports from thousands of independent dealers who sell Macmillan and more than 800 other brands of oil

Pan American Generals Tour U.S. Bases

At the invitation of our Secretary of War, generals from Pan American countries are touring United States camps and bases.

Airborne troops demonstrate their training exercises at Fort Benning, Georgia.

Mexico's defense minister shows particular interest in a flame-thrower. The generals agree that a modern army equipped with modern weapons will enable them to join in keeping the peace.

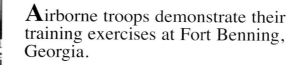

58

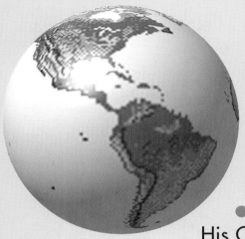

- Italy Grants Women Voting Rights.

- Italians Vote For Republic Form Of Government In First Free Election Since 1922— King Umberto II Leaves Italy.

- Emperor Hirohito Disclaims His Own Divinity.

- Japan's Former Premier, General Hideki Tojo And 27 Other Defendants Go On Trial In Tokyo For War Crimes.

- Emperor Hirohito Spared War Crimes Trial By Allies.

- Women Exercise Right To Vote In Japan For The First Time.

- U.S. Announces It Will Stay In Korea Until The Country Is Free And Unified.

- President Truman Pledges Aid For The Philippines As The Nation Becomes An Independent Republic.

- Soviet Union And Switzerland Resume Diplomatic Relations After 22-Year Break.

- Britain And France Withdraw From Syria.

- Ho Chi Minh Wins North Vietnamese Elections.

- French Government Declares Martial Law In Vietnam As Full-Scale War Becomes Imminent.

- 21-Nation Peace Conference Opens In Paris To Discuss Peace Treaties For Italy, Hungary, Romania, Bulgaria and Finland.

PALESTINE

Britain Imposes Curfew On Jewish Community In Tel Aviv Following Death Of Seven British Soldiers In Palestine.

Jewish State Rejected By The Anglo-American Committee Of Inquiry On Jewish Problems In Europe And Palestine.

Terrorist Organization Irgun, Under Leadership of Menachem Begin, Claims Responsibility For Attack On British Headquarters At King David Hotel In Jerusalem, Citing Suppression Of Immigration Of Jews.

British Troops Isolate Tel Aviv In Search Of Zionist Guerrillas.

Jewish Protestors Sing The Jewish National Anthem, "Hatikva," In Protest Over British "Operation Igloo," The Deportation To Cyprus Of Jewish Immigrants Seeking Refuge In Palestine From European Persecution.

Truman Urges Britain To Open Palestine To Jewish Refugees Who Immigrated Illegally Seeking Sanctuary From European Oppression And Throws His Support Behind A Jewish State. Arabs Accuse Him Of Betrayal.

London Conference On Palestine Boycotted By Jews And Arabs.

Divers and other salvage workers operate around the clock, taking advantage of low tides when water can be pumped out of the hulks.

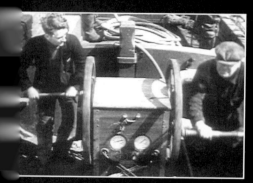

Post-War Salvage Operations Proceed Quickly To Clear Vital Shipping Lanes Of Sunken Ships In British Harbors

These pumps are capable of handling thousands of gallons of water a minute and have helped in the raising of hundreds of vessels.

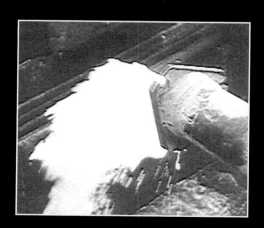

When the ship has been floated, it is towed to the nearest beach where further salvage operations are conducted.

Everything usable is saved for the rebuilding of Britain's shattered Merchant Marine.

On the other side of the North Sea is another ship graveyard filled with German wrecks.

The once powerful "Admiral Hitler" lies awash—a far cry from its days of glory.

Stalin Announces Five-Year Plan For U.S.S.R.

Moscow Denounces Churchill As Anti-Soviet Warmonger.

Winston Churchill Makes "Iron Curtain" Speech.

Soviet Spy Ring Uncovered In Canada.

Russia Agrees To Withdraw Troops From Iran. Accord Granting The U.S.S.R. 51% Control Of Oil For 25 Years Revealed By Tehran.

American Killed By Soviet Police For Photographing An Election In Berlin.

Bread Rationing Begins In Great Britain.

U.S. Charges The Soviet Union Of Stripping Hungary Of Needed Resources.

2.5 Million Pounds Of Clothing For European Relief Donated By New Yorkers.

President Truman Creates 9-Step Program To Feed Europeans.

Argentina's Col. Juan D. Peron Wins Sufficient Electoral Votes To Land Him Presidency. He Is Installed As 29th President Of Argentina.

Argentina And Soviet Union Resume Diplomatic Relations After 28-Year Break.

60-Day Siege Of War Declared In Chile.

Mao Tse-tung Orders Showdown With Chiang Kai-shek.

U. S. And China Sign Treaty Of Peace.

Mob Violence Escalates In Cairo As Egyptians Riot To Protest British Rule.

The British Flag Is Lowered For The Last Time In Cairo After 64 Years.

Greek King George II Restored To Throne In Referendum Landslide.

○ **HUNGARY PROCLAIMED A REPUBLIC.**

○ **60 INDIANS KILLED AND MORE THAN 500 INJURED IN BLOODY ANTI-BRITISH PROTESTS IN BOMBAY. 300,000 JOIN IN DEMONSTRATION.**

○ **ATTLEE OFFERS INDIA FULL INDEPENDENCE AFTER AGREEMENT ON CONSTITUTION.**

○ **NEHRU APPOINTED HEAD OF INDIA'S INTERIM GOVERNMENT.**

CHARLES DEGAULLE RESIGNS AS PRESIDENT OF FRANCE.

NOBEL PEACE PRIZE

Emily G. Balch & John R. Mott

HARLAN F. STONE, Chief Justice Of The United States, Dies At 73.

P
E
O
P
L
E

Margaret Rose, youngest daughter of Britain's King and Queen, makes her first public appearance by herself.

The Princess Goes Public

In the royal tradition, Princess Margaret visits a children's center.

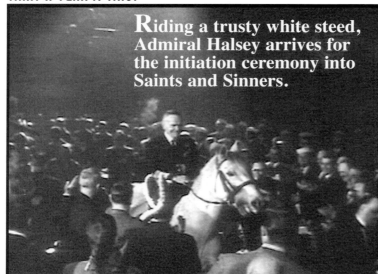

Riding a trusty white steed, Admiral Halsey arrives for the initiation ceremony into Saints and Sinners.

ADMIRAL HALSEY INITIATED INTO SAINTS AND SINNERS

General Doolittle and former President Battista of Cuba observe the festivities.

A rousing send-up of Hitler and Hirohito adds to the evening's festivities.

Admiral Halsey thanks the audience as he is formally welcomed into their group.

Mary Pickford,

America's First Lady of Film, receives a royal welcome on her arrival in London.

THE NEW GREY MARES AIN'T WHAT THEY USED TO BE

Despite Plunging Necklines, Winston Churchill's Columnist Son, Randolph, Declares That Women Aren't As Pretty As They Were And That All The Great Beauties Are In Florida.

Magazine Illustrators Dub Mrs. Elliot Roosevelt As Being  Among Those Having The Most Kissable Lips In America.

* Gertrude Stein Greets U.S. Writer, Richard Wright ("Native Son," "Black Boy") On His Arrival In Paris As A Cultural Guest Of The French Government.

Louis (r)

* Eva Peron Buys A $30,000 Carpet For The Presidential Home.

* The American Museum Of Natural History Adds A Sculpture Of Joe Louis' Right Fist To Its Comparative Anatomy Collection.

* World War I Hero, Alvin York, Strikes Oil Near His Home In Tennessee's Cumberland Mountains.

* Laurence Olivier And His Wife, Vivien Leigh, Make A Safe Crash Landing In The Connecticut Countryside After Their Plane Loses An Engine.

Shaw

* George Bernard Shaw, The World's Greatest Living Literary Figure, Turns 90.

* Beautiful Hollywood Star, Linda Christian Sentenced To Five Days In Jail For Speeding.

Roosevelt

* During A Radio Interview, Eleanor Roosevelt Says She Deplores Attempts To Make Men And Women Equal Instead Of Complementing Each Other.

* Eleanor Roosevelt Badly Bruised In Three-Car Collision After Falling Asleep At The Wheel Of Her New Lincoln Sedan.

COUPLING

John Huston & Evelyn Keyes

Prince Louis II (Ruler of Monaco) &
   Ghyslaine Domanget

Kitty Carlisle & Moss Hart

George Balanchine & Maria Tallchief

UNCOUPLING

Celeste Holm & A. Schuyler Dunning

Joe E. Lewis & Martha Stewart

George Abbott & Mary Sinclair

Boris Karloff & Evelyn Helmore

Joan Fontaine & William Dozier

Freddie Bartholomew & Maely Daniele

John Wayne & Esperanza Baur

Mervyn LeRoy & Kathryn Prest Byfield Spiegel

Elizabeth de Gaulle & Alain de Boissieu

Myrna Loy & Gene Markey

Artie Shaw & Kathleen Winsor

Olivia de Havilland & Marcus Goodrich

Cornelius Vanderbilt & Maria Feliza Pablus

Diana Barrymore & Bramwell Fletcher

Ann Sothern & Robert Sterling

Diana Barrymore & Bramwell Fletcher

Joan Crawford & Philip Terry

Jascha Heifetz & Florence Vidor Heifetz

Artie Shaw & Ava Gardner

Ann Dvorak & Leslie Fenton

George Vanderbilt & Lucille Parsons Vanderbilt

Oscar Homolka & Florence Meyer Homolka

Stirling Hayden & Madeleine Carroll

GRIEVOUS AND IRRECONCILABLE DIFFERENCES
OH YOU CAD!

Gloria Swanson Sues Her Fifth Husband For Support On The Grounds That:
- He drinks too much;
- She prefers living in her apartment on Fifth Avenue, but he wants to live at his place on Park Avenue;
- He prefers sleeping in an oversized bed, while she prefers twin beds;
- He never built the bathroom on their glass-bottom yacht.

How much does she want to be compensated for this dastardly behavior? $1,000 weekly to be exact!

PRINCESS ELIZABETH, HEIRESS TO BRITAIN'S THRONE, AND GREEK PRINCE PHILLIP ENGAGED BUT WEDDING PLANS DELAYED BY KING GEORGE VI DUE TO POLITICAL SITUATION IN ATHENS.

"WINNIE" RECEIVES WARM WELCOME IN NEW YORK

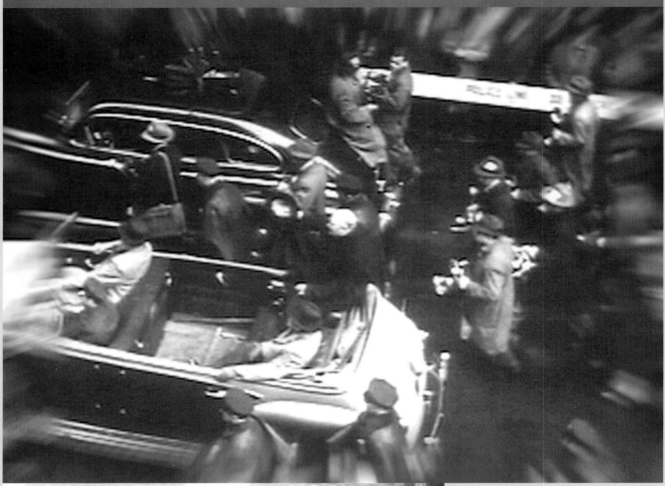

One of the original Big Three, Britain's former Prime Minister, Winston Spencer Churchill arrives in New York to deliver an important speech.

Newly-elected Mayor O'Dwyer greets Mr. Churchill, the man who led England to victory.

Dissenters gathered at City Hall are quickly subdued.

Speaking at an official dinner before a distinguished audience of 2,000, Mr. Churchill backs up his position that he does not believe that Russian rulers wish for war at the present time and that war is not inevitable or imminent.

CHURCHILL GOES TO MIAMI

Winston Churchill arrives in Miami for a well-earned 6-week vacation.

The former Prime Minister is a guest at the home of a friend in Miami Beach.

Mr. Churchill, accompanied by his wife, is host to a press conference during which he warns against too rapid a drift toward world collectivism.

New York's Postmaster, Albert Goldman, Personally Answers And Distributes Donated Gifts To The Neediest From The More Than 10,000 Letters Addressed To Santa Claus Each Christmas.

•

Movie Star Van Johnson Receives Fan Mail Mostly From Older Women Who Want To Play Matchmaker.

•

President Truman's Favorite Dinner: Steak And Baked Potato.

Actress June Knight Finally Receives Telephone After A Year's Wait And Sends Out "New Arrival" Announcements With Date, Time And Weight.

•

Former Barber, Perry Como, Cuts His Young Son's Hair.

•

John F. Kennedy Runs For First Political Office And Wins Election To The House By 78,000 Votes.

Most Glamorous Mothers In America
RITA HAYWORTH & LANA TURNER

Greer Garson

COME TO ME MY MELON-COD-DE BABY...

A sardine fisherman by the name of Vincent Sallecito was doing a day's work as an extra in a film being shot in Monterey Bay starring Greer Garson. A huge wave knocked the beautiful Miss Garson off of the rock on which she was sitting at which point the gallant Mr. Sallecito jumped in immediately and carried her to safety. Miss Garson was treated for cuts, bruises, and a sprained back at a local hospital while the fisherman had his moment of fame and a chance to hold one of the most beautiful women in America.

FOR I ONLY HAVE DOTS FOR YOU...

When "The Polka Dot Girl" Chili Williams Was Seen Dotless In Public, William Schiller, Known As "The Polka Dot King" Promptly Sued Her For Breach Of Contract Stating That Under The Terms Of Their Agreement She Is Required To Wear Nothing But Polka Dots.

HE'D GIVE YOU THE TIE OFF HIS NECK

Connecticut Publisher William J. Pape Admired Harry S. Truman's Silver-Streaked Black Bow Tie Who Loaned It To Him For An Evening.

HARRY CONOVER NAMES
America's Most Beautiful Women

1. *Anita Colby*
   (The Most Beautiful)
2. *Maureen O'Hara*
   (The Most Perfect Features)
3. *Ingrid Bergman*
   (The Prettiest Woman On Screen)

Jackie Cooper Returns Home After Serving A 26-Month Stint In The Navy.

Charles "Lucky" Luciano Sings His Way Out Of His 10-20 Year Sentence By Providing The United States With Information On Italy During The War And His Reward Is Deportation To The Old Country.

☞ Jean-Paul Sartre, Novelist, Playwright, Essayist, Prophet And Author Of The Bible On Existentialism, *"Being and Nothingness,"* Arrives In New York For Lecture Tour Including Engagements At Yale, Harvard and Princeton.

☞ George Bernard Shaw's Solution To Overpopulation: Every Woman Should Be Paid $8,000 By Her Man Before Bearing His Child.

☞ British Historian Arnold J. Toynbee Receives A $152,000 Grant From The Rockefeller Foundation To Write A World War II History Of International Relations.

☞ Haile Selassie Receives The Wendell L. Willkie Memorial Award From The Manhattan Based African Academy Of Arts And Research For His Contribution To International Peace And Good Will.

☞ Dr. Lise Meitner, Refugee German Physicist And Pioneer Contributor To The Atomic Bomb Is Chosen "Woman Of The Year" By The Women's National Press Club.

Harry S. Truman Wins Life Membership In The Society For The Preservation And Encouragement Of Barber Shop Quartet Singing In America, Inc.

Franklin D. Roosevelt's Stamp Collection Auctioned Off At New York Gallery.

"you bet I'm particular!
. . . I want my sodas in *DIXIE CUPS*"

"What I mean is—at fountains or other public places I don't like drinking out of something that another person has already used. An individual Dixie Cup has never touched any lips but mine. Take this soda...it *tastes* better in a Dixie Cup because you know it's *clean*."

Guy Lombardo Wins National Motorboat Sweepstakes In Red Bank, New Jersey Competition.

The International Sound Research Institute Gives Annual Award For Good Diction To Ingrid Bergman.

Playwright Thorton Wilder Is Made Member Of The Order Of The British Empire In Manhattan For His Help In Planning Combined Operations In The Mediterranean.

Benito Mussolini's Body Stolen From Pauper's Grave In Milan.

General Douglas MacArthur Receives The French Grand Cross Of The Legion Of Honor In Tokyo.

Mother Frances Cabrini, Founder Of The Order Of The Sacred Heart And America's First Saint, Is Canonized In Rome.

The Vatican Elevates New York's **Francis Spellman** To Cardinal.

SOMEONE'S IN THE KITCHEN WITH BESSIE

First Lady, Bess Truman, And Some Of Her Friends Don Aprons And Whip Up A Meal In The White House Kitchen For 70 Students Of The First Lady's Spanish Teacher.

Jimmy Walker, Mr. New York, Dies At 65.

Sinatra

Grable

Frank Sinatra And **Ingrid Bergman** Voted Least Cooperative Stars By Hollywood Newspaperwomen With **Betty Grable** And **Ginger Rogers** Tying For Second Place.

Shirley Temple's Brother, George, Wins First Match In His Wrestling Debut.

SOMETHING OLD, SOMETHING NEW, SOMETHING BORROWED ...ER...LET'S SKIP RIGHT TO SOMETHING BLUE

Newlywed Shirley Temple Turns Down Fan's Request To Borrow Her Wedding Gown, Stating That Some Things Have To Remain Personal And Sentimental.

HERE HE IS, MR. AMERICA

Alan Stephan, Ex-Sailor From Cicero, Illinois, Is Voted Mr. America.

The Miss United Nations Title Goes To Marjorie Bertha Morgenstierne, Daughter Of Norwegian Ambassador Wilhelm.

Mind If I Dunk?

Happy Felton demonstrates acceptable dunking practices with his hide-and-dunk *(left)* and donut-on-a-string *(right)*.

Some of his friends are for a more traditional approach of the straight dunk-and-bite method.

This dunker has developed the two-fisted dunk-and-bite approach guaranteed to double your dunking pleasure.

HUMAN INTEREST

She carries a nest of planes protected by gun batteries that were unheard of before the FDR was built.

The carrier Franklin D. Roosevelt, the mightiest warship afloat, makes her initial shakedown cruise. This 45-ton vessel was commissioned on Navy Day in honor of the late president.

The signal officer still plays a key role in bringing the Corsairs to safety.

NAVY TESTS NEW PLANE

The Navy tests newest post-war addition to its aerial defense weapons—the Douglas BT-2-D, a combination torpedo and dive bomber.

With a 2,500 horsepower engine and a cruising range of 1,500 miles, the latest weapon of defense is equipped with new diving brakes that slow it down to landing speed in seconds.

The Civil Aeronautics Authority Predicts That By 1955 One Family In 100 Will Own Its Own Plane.

Jet-Propelled Fighter Plane Sets Nonstop Transcontinental Speed Record Flying From Long Beach, California To La Guardia Field In 4 Hours 13 Minutes.

A Spokesman For The Agriculture Department Reveals The Development Of A Radio Proximity Fuse Which Will Allow Fire Fighters To Fight Forest Fires In The Future With Water Bombs Dropped From Large Bombers.

SLEEPING HABITS INTERPRETED

On Your Back ....Fearless
Stomach ....Intense
Curled Up ....Escapist
Hugging Your Pillow .Need Affection
Talk In Your Sleep ...Talk Too Much When Awake

Bell Telephone Predicts Long Distance Calls Will Be Processed As Quickly As Local Calls Within The Next 10 Years.

U. S. Post Office Predicts Speedy Future Airmail Service Through Use Of "Flying Mailcar" —Converted World War II "Flying Boxcars" Where Mail Would Be Sorted While In Flight.

Britain's Famed Physicist, Sir Edward Appleton, Predicts That Some Day The Mountains Of The Moon May Be Accurately Charted By Radar.

Rear Admiral Byrd Heads South Pole Expedition Involving 4,000 Men And A Dozen Vessels.

The Addition Of Bright Colors In Industrial Plants Seen As One Way Of Cutting Down On Accidents.

FAVORITE COLORS OF AMERICAN MEN

1. Blue
2. Red
3. Purple
4. Green
5. Orange
6. Yellow

New Cloud Meter Developed By General Electric May Allow Weather Forecasts Of The Future To Predict Amount Of Expected Rainfall.

A BIG DAY FOR DOGS AT THE WESTMINSTER DOG SHOW HELD AT NEW YORK'S MADISON SQUARE GARDEN

Proud owners show off their prized canines.

A
dog in a hat
is worth two
on a leash?

And the
champion is
*Hetherington
Model Rhythm*,
first Fox
Terrier to win
the Kennel
Club's top prize
since 1937.

Blessed with the best weather in 11 years, 75,000 people march up New York's Fifth Avenue in the annual St. Patrick's Day Parade.

The famous old 69th, the Fighting Irish, who distinguished themselves again in the last war, add a military note to the peace-time event.

THE LUCK OF THE IRISH

Among the more than a million and a half people watching the parade are the bishops *(right)* representing Cardinal Spellman, and Irish born and bred Mayor O'Dwyer and movie actor Pat O'Brien *(left)*.

President Truman Approves $2.4 Billion Bill For G.I. Leave Pay

I'M SO HUNGRY, I COULD EAT A HORSE... *AND DID!*

With the soaring price of meat making beef too expensive, New Yorkers have gotten on their high horse and have turned to eating Trigger's brothers and sisters. While former Mayor LaGuardia denounces this trend as being a sign of degeneration, Health Commissioner Weinstein states that horse meat is as nutritious and as good as any other meat.

With The Ending Of The War, Industrial Workers Have Less Incidences Of Indigestion, Insomnia, Fatigue, High Blood Pressure And Nervous Exhaustion.

THE COST OF WORLD WAR II: $680,000,000,000

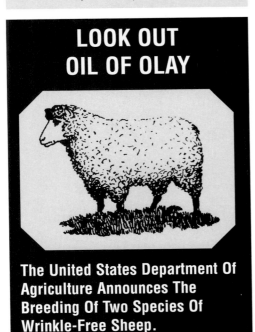

LOOK OUT OIL OF OLAY

The United States Department Of Agriculture Announces The Breeding Of Two Species Of Wrinkle-Free Sheep.

North Hollywood Pharmacy Calls Police To Handle Mob Who Snatch Up 2,000 Pieces Of Post-War Bubble Gum In Two Hours.

The Lord Mayor Of Bristol, Britain Welcomes The Banana Boat Tilapa Which Brings The First Bananas To Britain After Five Years.

Marines Land On Alcatraz To Quell Attempted Jail Break.

EASTER
SUNDAY
APRIL 21ST

The season's most popular messenger

Remember her on Easter with a Whitman's Sampler. She'll
be the proudest lady . . . proud of your thoughtfulness
in remembering her and remembering the day . . . proud,
too, of your excellent taste in choosing her dream candy,
the chocolates every woman knows are America's finest.

CRISP ALMONDS covered in thick, dark
gleaming chocolate . . . a rich delight
to bite into. One of the many taste
thrills in your Sampler.

Whitman's
CHOCOLATES

A WOMAN NEVER FORGETS THE MAN WHO REMEMBERS

Copr. 1946, Stephen F. Whitman & Son, Inc., Phila.

84

WANNA GET MARRIED?

HERE'S THE IDEAL QUALITIES TO LOOK FOR IN A MATE

The HUSBAND

Ambitious
Aware Of Social Problems
Common Interests
Considerate
Dependable
Desire For Children
Educated
Financially Secure
Good Character
Good Companion
Mentally & Physically Fit

Pressed Clothes
Religious Beliefs
Self-Assured
Sense Of Humor
Shined Shoes
Sincere
Supportive
Thoughtful
Tolerant
Trustworthy

The WIFE

Ages Gracefully
Cheerful
Combination Wife, Sweetheart & Mistress
Doesn't Make A Man Feel Married
Economical Dresser
Good Listener
Honest
Intelligent (But Not Smarter Than Her Husband)
Mutual Interests
Never Wears Bobby Socks
Sense Of Humor & Ability To Laugh At Herself
Unaffected

FROM "I DO" TO "I DON'T"

With more than 800,000 out of a total of 1,500,000 American war-wed GI's back in the States, the divorce rate has sky-rocketed with one out of every four of these often-times hasty marriages ending. Experts predict that two out of three wartime marriages will end in divorce by 1950.

A Woman In Camden, New Jersey, Is Granted A Divorce On The Grounds That Her Husband Made Her Duck Under The Dashboard Whenever He Drove Past A Girlfriend.

And In Salem, Massachusetts A Woman Sued For Divorce On The Grounds That Her Husband Was Too Affectionate And Stayed Home Too Much.

Navy Unveils Wartime Aerial TV Camera

An aerial television camera is loaded into a plane for a series of tests.

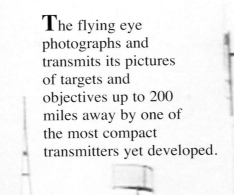

The flying eye photographs and transmits its pictures of targets and objectives up to 200 miles away by one of the most compact transmitters yet developed.

At a television room 40 miles away the images take shape on the screen, the kind of information that led to the sinking of Japanese ships in the Pacific.

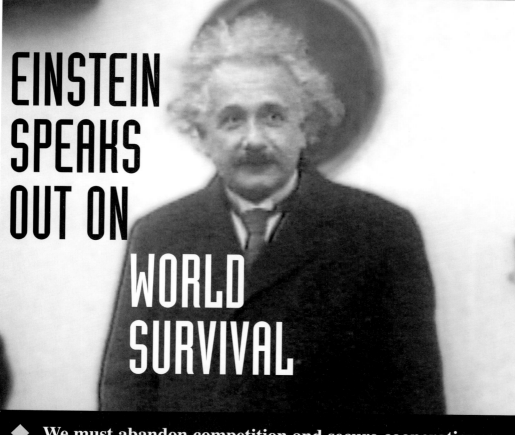

EINSTEIN SPEAKS OUT ON WORLD SURVIVAL

◆ We must abandon competition and secure cooperation vs. increasing size of armies.

◆ We cannot prepare for war at the same time we prepare for a world community.

◆ As long as we make bombs, we are also making hate and suspicion.

◆ Not even scientists completely understand atomic energy and the ultimate destructive capabilities of the bomb.

◆ The Emergency Committee of Atomic Scientists in Princeton, New Jersey was formed to disseminate information to the public as although science created this clear danger, the real problem is in the minds and hearts of men.

◆ We must realize that we cannot simultaneously plan for both war and peace.

◆ When we are clear in heart and mind—only then shall we find courage to surmount the fear which haunts the world.

Second Underwater Atomic Explosion At Bikini Sinks 10 Ships Including Battleship "Arkansas" And Carrier "Saratoga."

Albert Einstein Expresses Regret Over Use Of The Atom Bomb On Hiroshima.

Industrial Use Of Atomic Energy Explored.

Captain Eddie Rickenbacker Suggests An Atomic Bomb Be Dropped On The 1,800 Ft. Thick Antarctic Polar Icecap To Crack It Open.

THE AIR FORCE GETS READY FOR ATOM BOMB TESTS AT BIKINI ATOLL

Radio crews man ground instruments which send big flying forts into the air without pilots.

For the first time in history a crewless four-engine plane is handled by remote radio control.

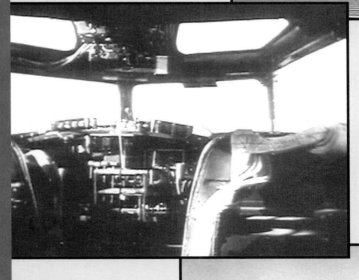

Destined for Bikini Atoll, a palm-studded island in the Marshall Islands, the battle-scarred B-17's are considered expendable.

BIKINI
ISLANDERS

are convinced to leave their home by the U.S. Government. A number of relocations ensue in the following decades, and the islanders endure starvation and extreme hardship. The people of Bikini remain scattered throughout the Marshall Islands while their old home awaits radiological cleanup.

American officials discuss evacuation plans with the natives.

The islanders say, "We will go believing that everything is in the hands of God."

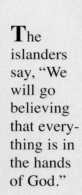

The precious Kona wood timbers of the community church are loaded onto boats.

Building materials including leaves for roofing are loaded onto boats along with personal belongings.

The women wave goodbye to their men who will return to get them after they build their new homes 109 miles away.

The Mayor Of Anchorage, Alaska Issues An Edict That Any Man Seen Without A Beard During The City's Fur Carnival Period Will Be Charged With Indecent Exposure.

The Average American Woman Spends Less Than $4.00 Yearly On Hats And Every Five Years Consumes Her Height In Lipstick.

Jitterbug Dancing Banned In A Ballroom In Sioux City, Iowa Due To Objections Over Bumps, Kicks And Jumps.

Metropolitan Life Insurance Company Reveals More Fatal Accidents Among Adults Occur In The Bedroom Than Any Other Room In The House.

According To Dental Authorities, The Majority Of Americans Don't Brush Their Teeth Regularly And Don't Even Own Toothbrushes.

Did you know that in Denver, a woman can't be photographed in a bathing suit without her permission and in England, it's against the law to marry your mother-in-law.

Meet Mohara...for <u>daylong</u> crisp appearance

First impressions count at any time of the year...never more so than in summer. Hot weather may be an alibi, but no longer an excuse for sloppy appearance. Now, smart grooming is easy, lasting and economical with the right fabric in your summer suit.

Through a most careful blending, Pacific has developed Mohara, a new, pleasantly cool tropical plus. Mohara combines all the natural advantages of worsted with mohair, the most resilient and lustrous of all animal fibres. There is added richness in Mohara's luxurious sheen...greater beauty in Mohara's silky, crisp appearance...longer staying power in Mohara's shape and crease retention...more wilt resistance to heat and humidity for daylong freshness ...plus colors that cool (determined by infra-red reflectance tests).

Joseph & Feiss' skilled tailoring has fashioned all these marvels of the fabric into suits that help you enjoy summer living at its cool, presentable best. Pacific Mills, Worsted Division, 261 Fifth Avenue, New York 16.

Available in limited but growing quantities at leading stores from coast to coast, single and double-breasted models **$32**

For further information write to the Joseph & Feiss Co., Cleveland 1, Ohio; or Pacific Mills, Worsted Division, Retail Service Bureau, 200 Fifth Avenue, New York 10.

FABRIC BY PACIFIC MILLS

MOHARA

REG. US PAT. OFF.

TAILORED BY JOSEPH & FEISS CO.

Pacific
Worsteds Woolens

THE COOL TROPICAL *plus* CRISP APPEARANCE

LOOK TO THE *Fabric* *FIRST—BUY PACIFIC*

According To An Article Published By The Population Reference Bureau, With The More Educated Sector Of The Population Having Less Children, The World Will Face A Shortage Of Brain Power.

Senator J. William Fulbright, Ex-Rhodes Scholar, Initiates Grants For Overseas Academic Exchange.

According To The U. S. Bureau Of The Census, Families Where The Wife Attended College Have Fewer Children.

The Bureau Of The Census Releases Figures Showing That Women Born In America To Foreign Or To A Combination Of Foreign And American Parents Not Only Marry At A Later Age Than Those Of American Descent But Are Less Likely To Marry At All.

WHAT PRICE FAME & GLORY?

According to a report in THE AMERICAN SOCIOLOGICAL REVIEW, Americans who achieve great enough prominence to be listed in WHO'S WHO are less likely to live as long as their unfamous contemporaries.

COUPLINGS & UNCOUPLINGS

MARRIAGES . .2,291,000
DIVORCES . . .610,000

ARRIVALS

BIRTHS 3,411,000

U.S. Birthrates Soar As Servicemen Return.

EDUCATORS AGREE THAT A THIRD OF ALL HIGH SCHOOL STUDENTS CAN'T READ OR WRITE WELL ENOUGH TO LEARN FROM TEXT BOOKS.

10,000,000 AMERICAN ADULTS REPORTED ILLITERATE ACCORDING TO STUDY CONDUCTED AT NEW YORK UNIVERSITY.

Liverpool, England Shipping Center Fights Series Of Unexplained Fires– Sabotage Suspected

A **German** warship, captured by the British Navy, is the latest of five vessels destroyed by fires of unknown origin.

Despite valiant fire-fighting efforts, this 17,000 ton craft destined to serve as a British troop ship becomes a gutted and charred wreck.

U.S. Treasury Marks 15th Anniversary of Series E Bond

Jeff Chandler makes a pitch for investing in government bonds.

Georgia's Governor Ellis Arnall Orders Legal Action To Revoke State Charter Of Ku Klux Klan.

Representatives from all faiths meet for National Brotherhood Week.

Former Governor Patton, Chairman, makes a plea for tolerance stating: *"It should be repeated time and again that anyone who lights the flame of bigotry or intolerance in America lights a fire underneath his own home."*

3,200 Protestant And Jewish Clergymen Representing Every State In The Union Endorse Planned Parenthood Services As A "Fundamental Democratic Right."

DIVERS PUT ON SHOW FOR WOUNDED VETS AT FLORIDA ARMY HOSPITAL

Divers go into action on a greased pole making it "Operation Slippery."

Variety

Celebrates Its 40th Birthday.

LIFE

Magazine Celebrates Its Tenth Anniversary.

Der Spiegel

Begins Publication In Hamburg.

The United Nations Educational, Scientific And Cultural Organization (UNESCO) Is Created.

The Statue Of Liberty Celebrates Her 60th Birthday.

Mexico City Builds The World's Largest, Most Modern Bull Ring.

First **CARE** Packages Arrive In France.

Pennsylvania Railroad Celebrates A Century Of Service To The American People.

- London's Heathrow Airport Formally Opens. Transatlantic Passenger Service To North America Begins Mid-Year.

- Shuttle Bus Service To Parking Facilities Begins In Chicago.

"But, darling, I'm going away <u>because</u> I love you!" cried Elsie

"DON'T PULL that old one on me," roared Elmer, the bull. "That's the same line you hand me every time you want to get your own way—and I'm not having any! What I want to know, woman, is where you're headed for and *why*."

"And I'll be delighted to tell you," cheerfully chirped Elsie, the Borden Cow. "I'm off on a flying tour of Borden's plants and laboratories."

"That's a hot one," haw-hawed Elmer. "And what in Cowdom Come will *you* do in a laboratory?"

"Oh, I won't *do* anything," answered Elsie. "I'm just going to watch my friends, the Borden scientists, do things. Dear, it's better than a magic show!"

"What! No rabbits?" sneered Elmer.

"Of course they have rabbits—in the *testing* labora-

HEMO HAS A NEW AND WONDERFUL "MILK-CHOCOLATE" FLAVOR!

tories for work on vitamins," smiled Elsie. "And speaking of vitamins, you'd be entranced with the *Hemo* plant! You could see how vitamins and minerals everyone needs every day are blended into a glorious *milk-chocolate* flavored drink. You could get a first-hand idea of vitamin control, too, when the scientists assay Hemo. You—"

"*Assay!*" exclaimed Elmer suspiciously. "What kind of foreign talk is that?"

"It's not just talk, dear," explained Elsie. "It's a very, very serious scientific procedure. A sort of check and double check on vitamin content. You know, the Borden folks are mighty particular about making everything as good as they say it is. For instance, when

MAKE GRAND SOUPS WITH BORDEN'S EVAPORATED MILK!

they say *Borden's Evaporated Milk* is rich in Vitamin D, you can bet your bottom dollar they're right—400 units per reconstituted quart! . . . Yes, dear, Borden's controls every single step in the preparation of its wonderful foods!"

"One thing they'll never control," groaned Elmer,

EXTRA-NOURISHING EXTRA-SAVORY BORDEN'S FINE CHEESES!

"and that's your tongue. Maybe *you* can control it long enough to tell me *exactly* where you're going?"

"Of course, dear," answered Elsie. "My first stop

will be to see the folks who make those delightful *Borden's Fine Cheeses*."

"Cheese!" drooled Elmer. "Why didn't you say so before? If I went along, do you suppose they'd let me do a little sampling on the side?"

"May-bee," doubtfully considered Elsie. "But, you know, Borden's has its own staff of cheese tasters and testers, men who have devoted lifetimes to creating grand cheese foods like Borden's Chateau—that's the one with the exciting, tangy Cheddar flavor. It's—"

CREAM IN EVERY VITAMIN-RICH SIP OF BORDEN'S HOMOGENIZED MILK!

"Quit it!" begged Elmer. "You're driving me crazy."

"You're not the only one," laughed Elsie, "who goes crazy about the wonderful foods Borden's makes. Folks all over the country, and up in Canada, too, certainly love them. They buy them, and buy them, and buy them again, year after year. All of which proves, dear, that quality counts."

"Quality—my eye!" argued Elmer. "It's *taste* that counts."

"But, dear, you can *taste* quality," soothed Elsie. "You taste it in every delicious, smooth sip of glorious *Borden's Homogenized Milk*. There's Vitamin D in every drop, you know. And every little globule of

GREAT TREATS ANY TIME BORDEN'S ICE CREAM AND MILK SHERBETS!

cream is broken into tiny particles and spread all through the milk."

"No matter how you spread it," sighed Elmer, "it's still Borden's. Woman, woman, can't you ever even *think* of anything but business?"

"Of course, dear," brightly twittered Elsie. "I *love* to think of fun and good times, too. And when I do, I think of *Borden's Ice Cream* and *Milk Sherbets*. They really make a party a *party*. And they're such good, nourishing treats *any* time."

"Any time, every time, *all* the time," wearily mumbled Elmer, "it's Borden's, Borden's, Borden's."

"Why, dear, you made a slogan!" enthused Elsie. "Almost as nice as our famous one—*if it's Borden's, it's GOT to be good!*"

— if it's Borden's, it's <u>got</u> to be good!

TUNE IN **GINNY SIMMS** IN A **GREAT RADIO SHOW** WITH **Comedy Guest Stars** FRIDAY EVENINGS - CBS

© The Borden Company

END OF THE RAINBOW

Thousands of people show up to say goodbye to the famous Rainbow Club in London, a Red Cross club that entertained 18 million GI's during the war.

Distinguished guest Eleanor Roosevelt, addressing the sentimental gathering, said:
"It is a sad day for many, because partings are always sad. But it is a joyous day too. The war is over, and men who came here for the war can now go home."

the last dance is danced at this

THE *Graduation Gift* EVERY CHILD <u>DESERVES</u>!

The gift that can mean better marks! If your child is being graduated from grammar school or high school . . . you can give no better gift to him or her than a *portable typewriter*.

For writing in longhand is slow and tiresome, often a big drawback to many bright-minded students.

This is a *fact!* Tests made by educators among thousands of school children reveal that when work is typed . . . *marks definitely improve!*

So give a Royal Portable as *your* graduation gift—and give your child a chance for *higher marks* next term!

17% more work is done! According to tests made by educators, typing turns homework into fun . . . notebook keeping into a pleasure instead of a chore . . . makes theme-writing easier, more enjoyable for your child. Helps him do *more* work, get *better* marks at the same time, too.

32% fewer errors in English! Educators have found that many mistakes in grammar, caused by carelessness, fairly leap from the typed page . . . are quickly caught by the student himself. In the same way, typing reduces careless spelling errors as much as 40%!

The right machine for your child! The Royal Portable is a regular office typewriter in portable size—with such work-saving features as these: (A) famous "Magic" Margin that makes margin-setting quick and easy. (B) Shift Freedom. (C) Speedy Finger-Flow Keyboard, standard in size and key slope. (D) "Touch Control" which adjusts to light or heavy touch.

Teaches independence! Many a child makes pocket money by typing correspondence, notes, and recipes for parents and friends. Older boys and girls often pay for their Royal Portables in this way. Quiet De Luxe Model shown, $66.74, plus tax. Also available, Arrow Model, $56.39, plus tax. All prices subject to change without notice.

The gift with a "future!" Learning to type at an early age often pays off later—in high school and college. When job-hunting time comes, typing knowledge helps, too! So see your Royal Portable dealer and order a Royal Portable now! P.S. If the model you want is not available, please be patient. A Royal Portable is well worth waiting for!

ROYAL
PORTABLE

<u>THE</u> standard typewriter in portable size

"Magic" and "Touch Control" are registered trademarks of the Royal Typewriter Co., Inc.

Americans Consume A Record 714 Million Gallons Of Ice Cream.

☆ According To The "AMERICAN FRUIT GROWER" The Banana Is A Berry But The Strawberry Is Just A Fruit.

☆ New York Christmas Shoppers Overrun Macy's And Gimbels' In Biggest Buying Spree In History.

Constant Bombardment Of Street Noises Thought To Be The Cause Of The Shrill, High-Pitched Voice Of The Average New Yorker.

Dutch Windmills Dwindle To 1,400—Down From 9,000 In The 1870's.

Murder Incorporated Hit Man "Bugsy" Siegel Builds The Flamingo Hotel In Las Vegas, Launching The Desert Town Into A Gambling Resort.

Brooklyn's Famed Coney Island Attracts As Many As One Million People On An Average Sunday Who Stroll The Widest Boardwalk In The World And Who Lose And Find Approximately 2,200 Children A Season.

PROFILE OF KILLERS

Older men who murder women usually do so to avenge acts of infidelity or unrequited love while younger men are more likely to kill other men instead of women and usually commit the crime during an argument.

MISS AMERICA:
Marilyn Buferd
(Los Angeles, California)

PASSINGS

PATTY SMITH HILL, Progressive Education Expert, Author Of The Verse "Happy Birthday," Dies At 78.

DR. FREDERICK L. HOFFMAN, Founder Of The American Cancer Society, Dies At 80.

How Many Miles Of Thread Does It Take To Dress A Man?

ITEM OF CLOTHING	NO. MILES OF THREAD
Underwear	9
Socks	2 1/2
Shirt	10
Tie	1
Suit	36

TOTAL MILES OF THREAD: 58 1/2 MILES

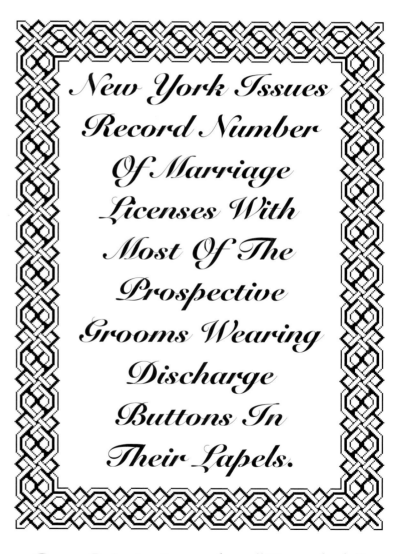

New York Issues Record Number Of Marriage Licenses With Most Of The Prospective Grooms Wearing Discharge Buttons In Their Lapels.

Great Britain Launches "Greenbelt" Program Which Is Designed To Create Garden Settings Within The Cities.

REPUBLIC SEABEE

FAIRCHILD F24R

JOHNSON ROCKET 185

GRUMMAN WIDGEON

CULVER MODEL "V"

AERONCA CHAMPION

BEECHCRAFT D18S

CESSNA 140

ERCOUPE 415C

HOCKADAY COMET

GLOBE SWIFT

LUSCOMBE SILVAIRE

WACO MODEL E

TAYLORCRAFT BC12D

STINSON VOYAGER 150

PIPER CUB SPECIAL

BELLANCA CRUISAIR SENIOR

NORTH AMERICAN NAVION

Here's why most Personal Planes are equipped with

CHAMPION
Spark Plugs

In personal planes the ultimate in dependable engine performance is a "must". Champion Spark Plugs are specified as standard equipment on the overwhelming majority of these engines and used by most private pilots.

Here once again is dramatic proof that Champions make every engine a better performing, more dependable engine. That's why dependable Champions are preferred in every field—why experts insist on them!

Insure championship performance and dependability in every engine you operate—automotive, aircraft or marine —by insisting on dependable Champion Spark Plugs.

CHAMPION SPARK PLUG COMPANY, TOLEDO 1, OHIO

THEY'RE DEPENDABLE!

FOLLOW THE EXPERTS . . . DEMAND DEPENDABLE CHAMPIONS FOR YOUR CAR

DISASTERS

CHICAGO:
Fire At
LaSalle Hotel
Causes 61
Deaths.

**NEW YORK
CITY: Fire
Destroys
Staten Island
Ferry
Terminal,
Causing
$2 Million
Damage And
Claiming 2
Lives.**

**NEW
YORK
CITY:
5 Killed
When
Army
Plane**

**Lost In
Fog
Crashes
Into
58th
Floor Of
Building
On Wall
Street.**

MOUNT TAKI,
the famed Japanese
crater on the southern-
most tip of Kyushu
Island erupts after being
dormant for 32 years.

Moving down the slope at the rate of 10 yards per
hour, the molten lava threatens everything in its path.

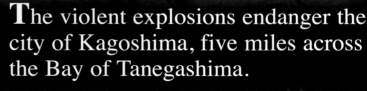

The violent explosions endanger the city of Kagoshima, five miles across the Bay of Tanegashima.

Villages on the crater side of the bay are evacuated and the inhabitants watch the fireworks from a safe distance.

HUNDREDS DIE AS TIDAL WAVE RIPS HAWAII

Worst Disaster Since Pearl Harbor

A series of giant waves, varying from 30 to 50 feet high, originating in submarine earthquakes off the Alaskan coast travelled 2,500 miles to Hawaii at an incredible speed of 300 miles per hour and struck in the early morning hours.

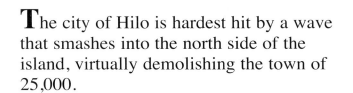

The city of Hilo is hardest hit by a wave that smashes into the north side of the island, virtually demolishing the town of 25,000.

With 90 people dead and many more unaccounted for, the army helps in rescue operations.

ILLINOIS: 46 Killed, 100 Injured When Second Section Of Express Train, Travelling At 75 MPH, Crashes Into Stopped First Section.

TURKEY: 1,330 Killed, Villages Leveled By Earthquake.

JAPAN: Earthquake Kills 1,088, Leaves Nearly 100,000 Homeless.

ENGLAND: 33 Killed, 500 Injured When Guard Rails Collapse At Football Stadium In Lancashire.

INDIA: 160 Pilgrims En Route To Ceremonial Bath Die When Temporary Jetties On Hooghly River Collapse.

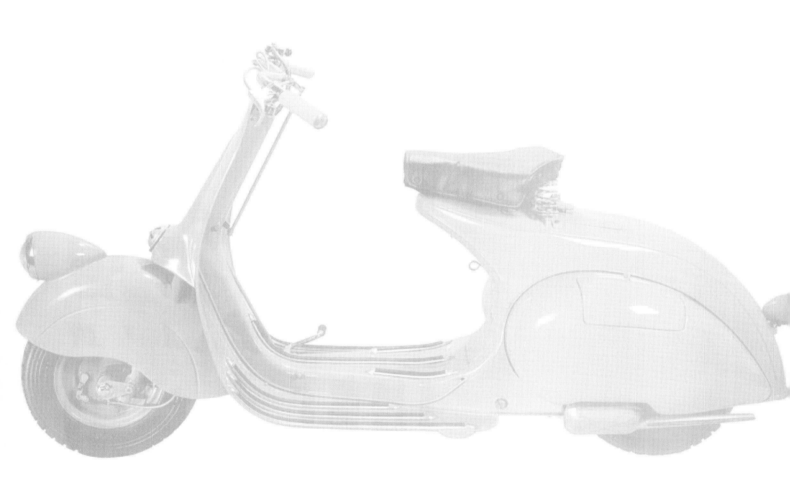

What's New

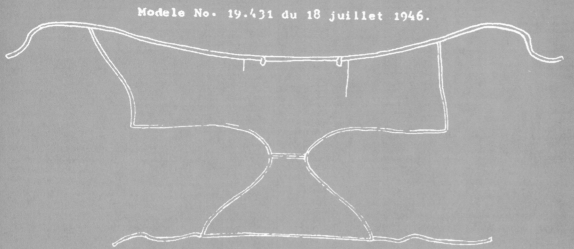

Modele No. 19.431 du 18 juillet 1946.

The modern bikini bathing suit is invented by automotive engineer Louis Reard in Paris, named for atomic bomb test site Bikini Atoll.

INVENTIONS

Electronic Brain Built At Pennsylvania University.

Chester Carlson Invents Xerography.

Grape Processing Machine Developed By Georges Monnet Of New York.

Ford Motor Company Engineer Delmar S. Harder Devises System To Manufacture Engines And Coins The Word "Automation."

Westinghouse Electric Corporation Introduces Most Brilliant Electric Lamp Ever Developed For Commercial Use.

IBM Develops Fast Electronic Calculator "ENIAC" For The U.S. War Department. Model For Commercial Use Ready For Release.

 Great Atlantic And Pacific Tea Company Solves Bread Mold Problem By Exposing Wrapped Bread To A High-Frequency Heat Generated In An Electric Oven.

The Dry Cleaning Industry Tries To Develop Technique For Cleaning Curtains And Draperies Made Of Fiber Glass

Eniac

Fairey Aviation Company Builds Pilotless Rocket Missile.

First Jet Fighter Plane Developed In Britain.

Self-Charging Portable Radio Designed To Operate For 20 Hours On A Penny's Worth Of Electricity Through The Use Of A 2-Volt Leak-Proof Rechargeable Battery Is Introduced.

B-17 Bombers Fly From Hawaii To California Without A Crew, Controlled Entirely By Radio.

General Electric Is Assigned Patent Rights To Refrigerator With Separate Ice-Cube Freezer Which Promises Greater Efficiency In The Development Of Tomorrow's Refrigerators Which Will Have Two Temperatures.

Pilot Ejector Seat Tested Successfully At Wright Field.

A Combination Automatic Radio And Electric Clock Replaces The Alarm Clock.

U.S. NAVY ANNOUNCES PLANS TO BUILD WORLD'S FIRST ATOMIC SUBMARINE

Rudolph F. Mallina Of Hastings-On-Hudson, New York Invents The Push-Button Telephone And Assigns Rights To The Bell Telephone Laboratories, Inc.

Mind If I Dunk?

The newest innovation for dunking a doughnut comes to us from Connecticut where a baker devised a doughnut with the usual hole in the middle but with a handle twisted like a cruller for an easy holding-and-dunking motion.

Anthony W. Delucchi Of Stockton, California Gets U.S. Patent On Design Of A Drive-In, Serve Yourself Restaurant.

General Electric And The Automatic Canteen Company Of America Develop An Electronic Vending Machine Which Dispenses Hot Food, Such As Hamburgers Or Hot Dogs For A Dime.

General Electric's "Traffic Master" Automatically Regulates Amount Of "Go" Time At Busy Intersections.

Hidden Automobile Burglar Alarm Developed By Fred E. Engler, Pukwana, So. Dakota.

Bell Telephone Announces Testing Of Mobile Radio-Telephone Service Along Three Interstate Highways.

Plane That Sheds Its Wings And Turns Into An Automobile Created By Aviation Engineer Ted Hall.

Start Easier! Amazing New Oil...War-Proved in Army and Essential Equipment

NEW Mobiloil

Makes Engines Cleaner...Perform Better...Last Longer!

Keep Your Engine Mobiloil Clean

1. "Mobiloil Clean" means that new improvements in Mobiloil keep rings, pistons, valves freer from deposits that waste power, fuel—vital working parts are cleaner.

2. New Mobiloil insures immediate oil distribution to all working parts—full delivery of liquid oil to heavily loaded bearings.

3. New Mobiloil permits quick starts—assures utmost protection against wear—provides efficiency and economy of operation evidenced by low oil and fuel consumption and minimum repairs.

New Mobiloil has been proved the hard way—in thousands of Army combat and transport vehicles—essential truck and bus fleets . . .

It's the finest Mobiloil ever made!

Don't just "change oil"—change to New Mobiloil at your Mobilgas dealer's.

SOCONY-VACUUM OIL CO., INC. and Affiliates: Magnolia Petroleum Co., General Petroleum Corporation of Calif.

TUNE IN "INFORMATION PLEASE"— MONDAY EVENINGS, 9:30 E.S.T.—NBC

inventions

New Electronic Device Measures Speed Of A Baseball.

American Machine and Foundry Co. Unveils Prototype Of Automatic Pinspotter, Beginning A Revolution In Bowling.

Transparent Mirror Allows An Observer To See His Reflection While Watching What's Happening On The Other Side Of The Pane.

New Device Which Translates Sound Into Visible Patterns Will Help The Deaf Learn To Speak.

Conveyor Belt Allows Rapid Unloading Of Cargo From Planes While In Flight.

Western Union Announces Plans To Replace Millions Of Miles Of Wire With Super High-Frequency Radio Beams.

GENERAL ELECTRIC CREATES LAMP THAT DUPLICATES ARTIFICIAL SUNLIGHT WITH TANNING AND WARMING CAPABILITIES.

New Lie Detector Invention Using Electrical Apparatus Developed By The Chicago Police Department.

Wright

Frank Lloyd Wright Unveils "Bizarre" Model For Manhattan's Guggenheim Gallery.

PASSINGS

John Baird Logie, Inventor Of "Televisor"
(First Instrument To Transmit Scenes By Wire Or Wireless), Dies At 58.

Carlton C. Magee, Inventor Of The Parking Meter, Dies At 73

You don't stay <u>first</u> *unless* you're <u>best</u>

1915

"They won't work, and I'll prove it!" said a Detroit automotive engineer in 1913.

So he put a set of Goodyear's new multiple-cord tires on his car and set out for Indianapolis. To his amazement, he arrived there with the tires as good as new. Determined to prove his point, he wheeled onto the Speedway and tired himself out trying to wear out the tires.

His experience, and that of other drivers, proved that Goodyear had developed a tire which went 7500 miles instead of 2500! A tire which gave *3 times* the mileage of other tires! A tire so much better that by 1915 Goodyear became America's largest selling tire, and Goodyear went into first place in tire sales.

1946

"Ordered off okay," read the tags on this set of today's Goodyears.

And here's what that "okay" means: In one of the most brutal, rugged road tests ever given—in a test which wore out lesser tires one after another—these Goodyears clicked off 51,000 miles at an average speed of 60 miles an hour, and *were taken off still "okay!"*

Special test tires? No, sir! They're exactly the same tough Goodyears you'll find at your dealer's! No wonder Goodyear holds its place as America's first-choice tire for the 31st consecutive year!

Two versions of the world's finest tire:

De Luxe Rib Tread   De Luxe All-Weather* Tread

*T. M. The Goodyear T. & R. Co.

<u>First</u>–every year for 31 years

GOOD/YEAR

More people ride on Goodyear tires than on any other kind

118

New Products

New Electronic Blanket Keeps Bed At A Constant Temperature All Night Long.

FULLY EQUIPPED, FACTORY-FABRICATED HOUSES SELLING FOR UNDER $6,000 WILL BE PRODUCED BY SHELTER INDUSTRIES OF NEW YORK.

HOME INTER-COMMUNICATION SYSTEM GIVES MOM A NEW WAY TO KEEP AN EAR ON BABY.

2-Story Collapsible Trailer Offers An Answer To The Nation's Housing Problems.

New Lower-Priced Automatic Dishwashers Are Produced In A Factory That Formerly Made Cores For Armor-Piercing Bullets.

MODERNISTIC NEW CARS

You said the engine is where??

These lovely ladies demonstrate the ease with which this car converts to a convertible.

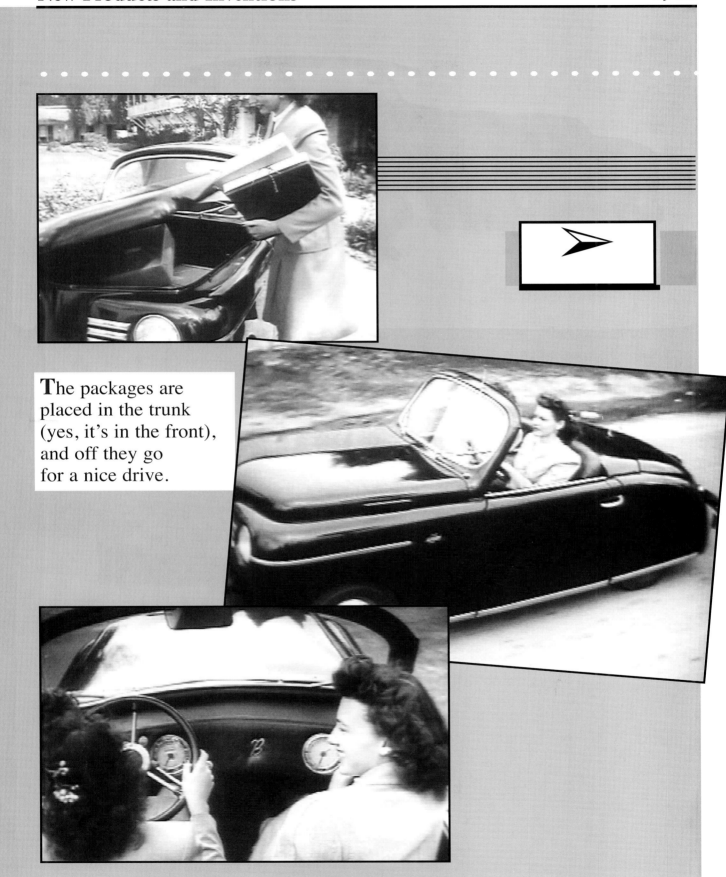

The packages are placed in the trunk (yes, it's in the front), and off they go for a nice drive.

KAISER
SPECIAL

PRODUCT OF KAISER-FRAZER

TRAIL BLAZERS

IN

POSTWAR STYLING!

BUILT AT WILLOW RUN

ONLY ONCE in a decade comes a distinctly new trend in motor car styling—a trend so clearly in accord with public preference that it is only a matter of time until all manufacturers fall into line. The KAISER SPECIAL and the FRAZER, America's first 1947 motor cars, have set a trend in body styling, passenger comfort and driver convenience that will be reflected in other automobiles in the years to come. You can see *these* cars at your dealer's showroom now.

FRAZER

PRODUCT OF
GRAHAM-PAIGE

Window That Opens And Closes Like A Venetian Blind Designed By Hardin Manufacturing Company Of Los Angeles.

Claiming DDT Coated Wallpaper To Be Non-Hazardous To Human Beings And Domestic Animals, The Trimz Company Of Chicago Develops Line Of Wall Coverings Coated With DDT Guaranteed To Be Effective Against Insects For A Year.

New Products

Lightweight Fiber Glass Material Developed As Insulation For B-29's May Be Used As Lining In Jackets, Mittens And Sleeping Bags.

"Airtopia" System Developed By Drayer-Hanson Of Los Angeles Heats Or Cools, Cleans, Humidifies, Or Dehumidifies, And Circulates Air For Homes And Office Buildings.

Saks Fifth Avenue Buys Newly-Developed Estee Lauder Cosmetics.

Kaiser-Frazer Automobiles Are Introduced.

In all this new postwar world—

only the New Chevrolet brings you
Chevrolet's famous BIG-CAR QUALITY at lowest cost!

THE moment you see this beautiful new Chevrolet you'll know that Chevrolet has again kept faith with its millions of owners and prospective owners by giving them Big-Car quality at lowest cost in purchase price, operation and upkeep.

You'll recognize this Big-Car quality in the many vital features found only in Chevrolet and higher-priced cars, and also in *every* phase of Chevrolet design and construction.

Big-Car quality guides the selection of the basic materials. Big-Car quality governs all Chevrolet specifications. Big-Car quality

guards every manufacturing operation, every inspection, every test. And, of course, such quality means much to you—and to us.

To you, it means deep and abiding satisfaction with your motor car investment; and to us, it means a steady continuation of that long-term friendship and favor which you and millions of other buyers have given to Chevrolet.

Decide now to get Big-Car styling, Big-Car comfort, Big-Car quality, by purchasing a new Chevrolet—the *only* low-priced car with all the Big-Car quality features illustrated here.

CHEVROLET MOTOR DIVISION. *General Motors Corporation*, DETROIT 2, MICHIGAN

NEW CHEVROLET

YOU PUT IT FIRST IN SALES

CHEVROLET

WE KEEP IT FIRST IN VALUE

NEW BEAUTY-LEADER STYLING *with modern, streamlined, Door-Action fenders,* featuring new Wide-Wing radiator grille; new hood ornamentation; sparkling new color harmonies; and massive new "Car-Saver" bumpers, giving "round the fender" protection, both front and rear.

PROVED VALVE-IN-HEAD THRIFT-MASTER ENGINE

exclusive to Chevrolet in its price range, and giving an unequaled combination of performance and economy.

LUXURIOUS BODIES BY FISHER
with No Draft Ventilation

with smart, modern lines and contours, with roomy, richly upholstered interiors and with Concealed Safety Steps —by far the most beautiful and most comfortable bodies in the entire low-price field.

POSITIVE-ACTION HYDRAULIC BRAKES

for smooth, safe, positive stops.

EXTRA-EASY VACUUM-POWER SHIFT
with Syncro-Mesh Transmission

the simplest, quickest and easiest of all steering-column gearshifts.

UNITIZED KNEE-ACTION RIDE

giving riding smoothness and riding comfort exclusive to Chevrolet in the low-price field.

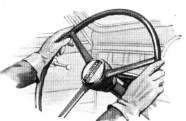

SHOCKPROOF STEERING

adding greatly to driving ease, driving comfort and driving safety.

NEVER HAS CHEVROLET BUILT A BETTER CAR THAN THIS **NEW CHEVROLET**

125

New Products

Eastman Kodak Introduces Ektachrome — The First Color Film A Photographer Can Process Himself.

Tide's In ... Dirt's Out

Procter & Gamble Introduces *Tide* To The Housewives Of America.

Vespa Motor Scooters Introduced In Italy.

☐ The New Westinghouse Laundromat Is A Front-Loading Machine Requiring Low-Sudsing Soap Or Detergent.

☐ Electric Clothes Dryer Hits The Consumer Market.

AT&T Announces Car-Phone Service In St. Louis.

STILL TICKING AFTER ALL THESE YEARS...
Norwegian-American Entrepreneur Joakim Lehmkuhl, Wartime Producer Of Timing Mechanisms For Bomb And Artillery Shell Fuses, Introduces Timex Watches.

AND...

H. Hattori & Co. Present Seiko Watches.

SCIENCE & MEDICINE

UNEXPLORED AREAS IN SCIENCE

- ✦ Living Longer, Healthier Lives
- ✦ Virus Conquests
- ✦ Psychological Disorders
- ✦ Exploration Of The Elements
- ✦ Exploration Of The Universe
- ✦ The Secret Of Photosynthesis
- ✦ The Secret Of Protoplasm
- ✦ Automatism
- ✦ Converting Psychological Warfare Into Psychological Welfare

■ The U.S. War Department Releases Report On Plans To Combat And Undertake Biological Warfare.

■ Rocket Engines Come Into Widespread Use In Experimental Aircraft And Guided Missiles.

NOBEL PRIZES

PHYSICS	MEDICINE	CHEMISTRY
Percy Williams Bridgman, For Work In High-Pressure Physics, U.S.	Hermann J. Muller, For Study Of Mutations Under The Influence Of X-Ray Radiation, U.S.	James B. Sumner, John H. Northrop, Wendell M. Stanley, For Work On Enzymes, All U.S.

Medicine

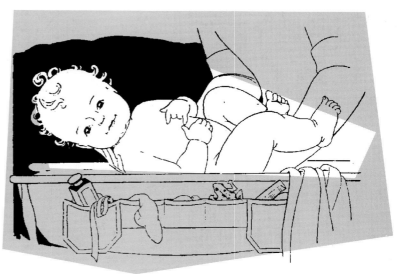

◆ Dr. John Adriani, Head Of The Department Of Anesthesia At New Orleans' Charity Hospital, Develops New Procedure That Eliminates Painful Childbirth Through Injection Of Anesthesia Into Spinal Canal.

◆ Toads Replace Rabbits In Pregnancy Tests As They Give Results In Four Hours Instead Of Forty-Eight.

◆ Immunization Shots Against Whooping Cough And Diphtheria Recommended In The Last Trimester Of Pregnancy To Insure Immunity In The Newborn Against These Diseases During First Months Of Life.

◆ New Test Developed To Determine Pregnancy Through Monitoring Variation In The Body's Morning Temperature.

Rheumatic Fever
1 **Number One Child Killer.**

Get Rid Of Those Saltshakers

✦ Salt Reduction Thought To Be Treatment For Stress Related Disorders.

✦ Recent Experiments Indicate That A Salt-Free Diet Will Help Some High Blood Pressure Patients.

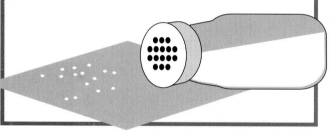

Vitamin Deficiency Studies Conducted By Council On Foods And Nutrition Of The American Medical Association Reveal Symptoms of Such Deficiencies.

Medicine

Coffee, Maple And Vanilla Ice Cream Found To Be Excellent Sources Of Carotene And Riboflavin.

Research Lab Releases Report Indicating DDT Spraying Of Dairy Cattle Pastures May Cause The Milk To Be Poisonous.

U.S. Chemist Vincent Du Vigneaud Synthesizes Penicillin.

•

Penicillin Gains New Stature As A Remedy Against Infectious Disease.

•

Penicillin Used Successfully In Curing Cattle Disease.

Food And Drug Administration Puts New Labeling Regulations Into Effect To Protect Consumers From Unsafe Non-Prescription Medicines.

HEADACHES ARE THE MOST COMMON REASON FOR SEEING A DOCTOR.

Hay Fever Sufferers Not Necessarily Neurotic

SNIFF SNIFF SNIFF

Dr. Earl R. Loew Discovers Benadryl, A Drug Which Brings Fast Relief For Hay Fever Sufferers And Victims Of Asthma And Hives.

Cancer Killed Twice As Many Americans As World War II.

Scientists Discuss Possible Link Between Smoking And Cancer At University Of Buffalo Symposium.

One Out Of Every Six Americans Is Infected With Trichinosis.

War Is Psychological Hell

- Psychological Study Released By The U.S. Army Indicates Psychiatric Casualties Are As Inevitable As Gunshot And Shrapnel Wounds And That Almost All The Men Who Fought In The North African Theatre Who Were Not Otherwise Disabled Ultimately Became Psychiatric Casualties.

- Paintings And Drawings By Battle Fatigued Veterans And People In Disturbed Psychological States Ignored In Clinical Research.

NURSES' DISCOVERY WINS GRATITUDE OF MILLIONS — THE WORLD OVER !

What is the secret of the fabulous success of the "little blue jar" that you see everywhere—in millions of homes—in first-aid stations at beaches—in dressing rooms of Broadway stars —in barber shops—in army barracks all over the world? Here is the amazing story!

NURSES were among the first to discover the secret! Discovered that Noxzema is good for *so many* different things! Discovered that this soothing, snow-white, medicated cream brought quick relief to hands made rough and red by frequent washings—cooling comfort to burning, tired feet and to chafed, irritated skin—quick relief to unattractive, blemished complexions.

The news spread—until today, in millions of homes, Noxzema has become a "family first aid" for minor burns and scalds, for sunburn, for baby's diaper rash and chafing, for father's shaving irritations and many other externally-caused skin troubles. Thousands of girls use Noxzema as a night cream and powder base to help rough, dry skin become softer and smoother—free from ugly surface blemishes.

How does Noxzema do so much? It's a *medicated formula*—soothing, cooling, comforting—aids in faster healing. And it's greaseless—doesn't stain clothes.

Over 25,000,000 jars of Noxzema are used yearly in the U.S.—millions more in Canada and other countries. Perhaps *you* are one of its loyal friends. If not, *try* it. Sold at all drug counters.

GIRLS WITH "PROBLEM SKIN" find Noxzema *so* effective in helping heal ugly, externally-caused blemishes and for softening rough, dry skin. Thousands use it as a protective foundation.

RED, ROUGH, HOUSEWORK HANDS worry many a housewife. Thousands keep a jar of Noxzema in the kitchen to smooth and soften hands, help heal painful chapping and minor burns.

MOST POPULAR SUNBURN PREPARATION in America, Noxzema brings glorious, cooling, soothing relief to the red, tender skin; it's greaseless, non-sticky—doesn't stain clothes or bed linen.

The fascinating 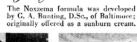 *story of Noxzema*

The Noxzema formula was developed by G. A. Bunting, D.Sc., of Baltimore; originally offered as a sunburn cream.

DURING THE WAR, MILLIONS of men found Noxzema a real friend in need, bringing comfort to tired, burning feet, to skin burned by tropical suns, chapped by arctic winds, made raw and sore in wet, insect-infested jungles.

Nurses were the first to discover many new uses for Noxzema; today surveys indicate that 7 out of 10 nurses use Noxzema for themselves or patients.

For years, First-Aid Hospitals at Atlantic City, Coney Island, Miami, and other big beaches have made Noxzema a standard treatment for sunburn.

Barbers first used Noxzema as a base for lather for customers with tough beards—tender skin. Now there is a special Noxzema Shave Cream for hard-to-shave men.

Surveys show that 8 out of 10 Broadway show girls interviewed use Noxzema for soothing skin relief, to combat effects of make-up and to help keep complexion smooth, clear and attractive.

NOXZEMA MEDICATED SKIN CREAM

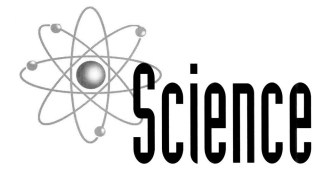

Science

The War Department Announces The Availability Of Radioactive Isotopes For Medical And Biological Research.

Glass Heart Tested On Laboratory Rats

DISCOVERIES

Underwater Islands Discovered Rising From Ocean Floor In The Pacific Between Hawaii and Marianas.

"Grand Canyon" Discovered In Mississippi Five Miles Wide With Walls More Than 600 Feet High.

Research Reveals The Blood From Thoroughbred Horses Differs From Ordinary Horses.

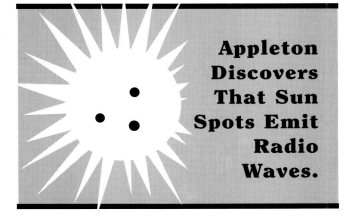

Appleton Discovers That Sun Spots Emit Radio Waves.

SOVIET SCIENTISTS CLAIM THEY SPLIT THE ATOM.

Isotope Carbon 13 Discovered.

Hear that Click?
A NEW POINT-INSTANTLY!

C·L·I·C·K
C·L·I·C·K

Press the Magic Button with your thumb—
EVERSHARP REPEATER PENCIL
Feeds New Points Like a Machine Gun

AN EVERSHARP Repeater Pencil not only speeds your writing... it speeds your very thinking! There's no twisting or turning, no messy lead handling. It's a one-hand operation. Just press the Magic Button and it feeds new points automatically from a six months supply—that you drop in the barrel just as easily as dropping sugar into coffee!

New featherweight construction ends fin-

ger strain—gives perfect balance for easier writing. EVERSHARP Repeater Pencils are priced from $1.50 to $50.
(Plus Federal Tax on pens $5 and over.)

Service Guaranteed Forever. If Your EVERSHARP Ever Needs Service, We Will Put It In Good Order For 35¢. This Service Is Guaranteed—Not For Years—Not For Life—But Guaranteed Forever!

TUNE IN Phil Baker in "TAKE IT OR LEAVE IT" —CBS, Sunday Night and EVERSHARP's Sensational New Show—Ann Sothern in "MAISIE" CBS, Wednesday Night.

Makes Every Mechanical Pencil Write Better
BUY EVERSHARP LEAD

15c
Desk Pack 10¢
Thrift Pack 25¢

Look for the package with the RED TOP

Fits All Mechanical Pencils
All sizes, grades and colors. Smoothest, Blackest, Strongest lead in the world.

Never Say "LEAD"
Say EVERSHARP LEAD

Give EVERSHARP_and you give the finest!

© 1946, Eversharp, Inc.

134

It's A Living

Department Of Agriculture Orders U.S. Bakers To Reduce Size Of Bread Loaves And Rolls.

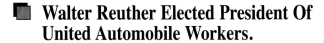

- Walter Reuther Elected President Of United Automobile Workers.

- Conviction Of Three U.S. Tobacco Companies For Violation Of Antitrust Act Upheld By The U.S. Supreme Court.

- Sharp Rise in Butter Prices Seen After U.S. Government Ends Its Subsidy.

- The Dow-Jones Industrial Average Reaches Post-1929 High Of 212.50 But Falls To 163.12.

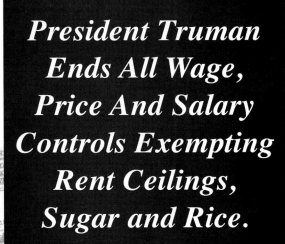

President Truman Ends All Wage, Price And Salary Controls Exempting Rent Ceilings, Sugar and Rice.

U.S. Farm Prices Reach Highest Level Since 1920.

A & P Food Chain Convicted Of Monopoly Acts.

MEAT PACKERS STRIKE PARALYZES NATION'S MEAT SUPPLY

More than a quarter million packing house workers strike across the nation for higher wages.

Negotiations between union, government and packing officials fail to produce an agreement, forcing the government to step in and take over.

The formal seizure notice is posted and union leaders order the strikers back to work.

The American flag is raised over seized plants and assembly lines in slaughter-houses begin full operations.

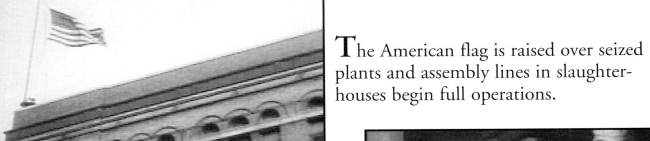

WORST WORK STOPPAGE SINCE 1919 SWEEPS THE UNITED STATES

JANUARY

7,000 Western Union Workers Walk Off Job, Paralyzing Telegraph Services In New York.

200,000 Members Of United Electrical Radio And Machine Workers Of America Walk Off Jobs In 16 States Halting Production Of All Appliances.

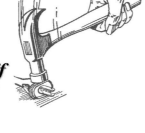

800,000 Pittsburgh Steel Workers Join Millions On Strike.

FEBRUARY

Mayor O'Dwyer Declares State Of Emergency As Striking Tugboat Workers Cripple New York.

10,000 Striking Philadelphia Transit Employees Paralyze City Transportation.

FEBRUARY / MARCH

STRIKE SETTLEMENTS REACHED AT FORD, GENERAL MOTORS AND GENERAL ELECTRIC.

APRIL

Approximately 400,000 Soft Coal Miners Strike.

MAY

U.S. Government Seizes Railroads To Avert Strike Which Commences Anyway.

John L. Lewis Settles 45-Day Coal Strike In White House Negotiations.

SEPTEMBER

Truck Strike Hits New York, Curtailing Deliveries Of Food.

Shipping Stops On All Coasts As Worst Maritime Strike In History Hits The U.S.

OCTOBER

First Strike In Airline History Staged By 1,400 Pilots And Co-Pilots Of Transcontinental And Western Air, Inc.

DECEMBER

U.S. Government Indicts John L. Lewis For Contempt And Fines Him $10,000 And United Mine Workers $3.5 Million.

this was the price that was

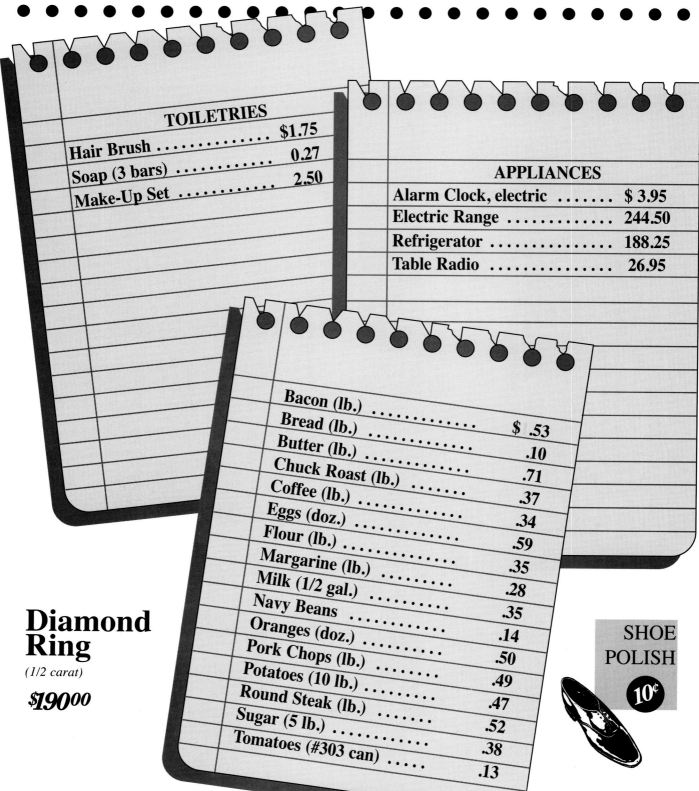

TOILETRIES

Hair Brush	$1.75
Soap (3 bars)	0.27
Make-Up Set	2.50

APPLIANCES

Alarm Clock, electric	$ 3.95
Electric Range	244.50
Refrigerator	188.25
Table Radio	26.95

Bacon (lb.)	
Bread (lb.)	$ .53
Butter (lb.)	.10
Chuck Roast (lb.)	.71
Coffee (lb.)	.37
Eggs (doz.)	.34
Flour (lb.)	.59
Margarine (lb.)	.35
Milk (1/2 gal.)	.28
Navy Beans	.35
Oranges (doz.)	.14
Pork Chops (lb.)	.50
Potatoes (10 lb.)	.49
Round Steak (lb.)	.47
Sugar (5 lb.)	.52
Tomatoes (#303 can)	.38
	.13

Diamond Ring

(1/2 carat)

$190⁰⁰

SHOE POLISH

10¢

Bridal Gown

$650.00

Women's •CLOTHING•

Bra	$ .79
Girdle	6.95
House Dress	1.95
Shoes	6.50

Men's Clothing

Hat	$ 12.50
Shirt	2.59
Shoes	10.50
Suit	27.00
Tie	3.50

SPORTS

Golf Bag and Clubs
$203.00

Tennis Racket
$22.00

Convertible
Station
Wagon
$2,890⁰⁰

This was a day in a dream

CHRISTMAS was today.

As long as I live I'll never forget this moment at the end of Christmas. The snow standing down there on our porch roof like a good meringue...the quiet twinkling stars (really twinkling).

And here, inside, this warm happiness stretching out under everything. Little Dickie tucked in bed between Old Mr. Teddy and New Mr. Teddy.

And Dick...just downstairs checking the lights and the fireplace...*not* on the high seas as he was *last* Christmas. What a thin gray day...with very sharp edges!

But today has been heaven...our house full of sunshine and talk and love and new toys

and more of our beautiful silver! Two new place settings in our own International Sterling pattern...now our set is complete!

How dear of Dick to think of it. I wrote him once that every time I set our table, the silver he and I had selected together was a sort of bridge...between the days when he was home and the time he'd be home again.

We have always been so proud of our International Sterling. So glad we selected the very best from the beginning. Dick couldn't have given me anything today that would have meant more—it's as though he had begun writing Part Two to our happiness.

Whenever you choose your "family" silver,

ask to see the International Sterling patterns.

Choose that one with your heart. As long as you live you'll enjoy its silver-solidness; the fine balance of each piece; the clear, beautiful design. Begin, if you like, with individual place settings: a knife and fork, teaspoon, salad fork, cream soup spoon, and butter spreader.

Prices on famous International Sterling have not been raised, even in the face of general rising prices. 6-piece place settings for as little as $21.50. All these patterns are made by The International Silver Company in the U. S. A.

TUNE IN to *The Adventures of Ozzie and Harriet*, Sunday Evening, 6:00 P. M., E.S.T., Columbia Broadcasting System.

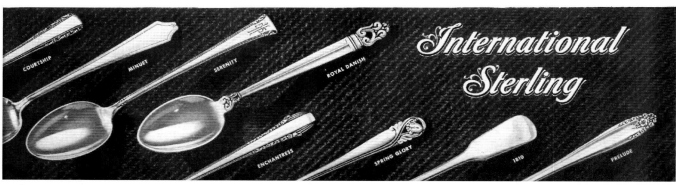

this was the price that was

• •

AIRLINE FARES
FOR 1946

San Francisco to Boston	$125.10
New York to Los Angeles	118.30
Los Angeles to Chicago	85.45
Dallas to New York	66.15
Detroit to Oklahoma City	44.70
Washington, D.C to Chicago	27.25
Los Angeles to Phoenix	17.10
Toronto to Buffalo	3.20

Miscellaneous

Billfold, Ladies' . . .	$4.50
Billfold, Men's	.5.00
Fountain Pen, Gold Tipped	.3.50

Household Items

Ironing Board	$ 6.95
Cedar Hope Chest	39.50
Blanket	6.45
Sheets	2.35
Sterling Silverware (6-piece place setting)	23.00

• •

PASSINGS

JOSEPH MEDILL PATTERSON,
Founder Of The New York Daily News, Dies at 67.

ARTHUR CHEVROLET,
One Of Three Swiss Brothers Who Made Automotive History, Dies at 61.

MERRITT CUTLER

The last lovely touch to a lovely Boudoir . . .

Jewelite

PRACTICAL as they are beautiful, Jewelite combs, brushes and complete dresser sets will be cherished by every woman who cares for lovely things. Available in sparkling crystal or precious jewel colors, each article comes packaged in its own miniature showcase of transparent plastic. Ask for Jewelite at any good brush department. There are many kinds and grades of plastic, so be sure you get *genuine* Jewelite, the aristocrat of plastics. Pro-phy-lac-tic Brush Company, *Florence, Mass.*

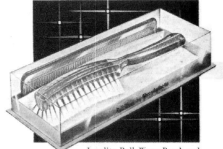

Jewelite Roll-Wave Brush and Comb in delicate shades of ruby or sapphire, or diamond-clear crystal.

JEWELITE BY PRO-PHY-LAC-TIC

The fashion industry meets the challenge of lavish social activities and using materials scarce during the war such as silk, satin, linen and lace produces some of the most elegant, luxurious clothing seen since the Roaring 20s. American designers scale the heights in ingenuity and receive international recognition for their creations.

FASHION

The American Female – The Look

This suit combines a beige jacket with dark brown skirt.

A copper-colored wool using diagonal closing.

The look ranges from hip-length jackets, squared at the shoulders to shorter jackets with sash ties to rounded at the shoulders narrowing at the waist and hips.

Long Skirts Legalized With The Repeal Of Austerity Measure L85.

With the introduction of the strapless bra, the new bare-shouldered look becomes the fashion for evening.

With Their Men Now Back From The War, Women Spend A Record $1.5 Billion For Their Easter Outfits.

Straw hats return for the first time since the war began and are trimmed with flower, feather and jewel decorations.

146

A "MALLORY MATCH" Makes Time!

Inside this coat of smart sports plaid
You'll be a happy gent, m'lad.

Just park this lightweight felt aloft
And make the stoniest heart turn soft

Brunettes or blondes, they're all the same,
When a "Mallory Match" applies the flame!

The Dallas $15.00
IN PLIAFELT

● The way she looks *at you* depends on how you look *to her!*
So start that important week end right, with a good-looking suit and carefully matched accessories. And be sure to top off your outfit with a handsome DALLAS by Mallory.

You'll discover this all-American lightweight with a Texas accent has everything it takes. It's made in *Pliafelt*, too—Mallory's exclusive process that makes a hat superbly soft and crush-resistant.

Visit your Mallory dealer soon to select *your* DALLAS.

At fine men's stores everywhere

MALLORY
hats
STYLE LEADERS FOR 129 YEARS

Two ways to show up to advantage

1. The two men above are headed in different directions, but they'll both show up looking their best.

To do as well by yourself, you needn't have a house full of clothes, or even spend a lot of money. Just pick your clothes sensibly, with an eye to where you'll wear them.

Then, when you're headed for a big time, as these two are, you'll be set with an outfit that's right for the occasion —even to a smart new Stetson Narrow Brim hat...

2. The lad on the left is out to meet his date in a single-breasted, blue-gray sharkskin suit. His crisp blue-and-white striped shirt sets off his blue polka-dot tie to a T. And the crowning touch is one of the new Stetson Narrow Brim hats, blending quiet, good taste with a youthful air. This Stetson is the Vogue, in popular Caribou Gray.

3. The gent with the girl is headed for a party carrying a light brown diagonal-weave topcoat, and wearing a double-breasted dark brown suit with a narrow pin stripe. His shirt is white—his tie, a lively small print of red, black and yellow. The hat is the distinguished Stetson Diplomat, with narrow brim, in handsome Arabian Brown.

STETSON Narrow Brim Hats — Right for dressing up

The American Male— The Look

Men's fashion is predominantly still conservative in its look consisting of dark gabardine suits and sack coats without vests. More elaborate patterns and brighter colors are used in the newer worsted suits. Hats are narrow brimmed with high crowns.

Apparel Arts Names Best Dressed Sailor
Fleet Admiral Ernest J. King

Newest headbands for bangs: black lace on black velvet ribbon, decorated with bows.

With Nylon Material Being Less Scarce, The Nylon Dress Which Does Not Require Ironing After Washing, Becomes Popular.

French Couturier Louis Reard Introduces Two-Piece Bikini Which Is Banned At Biarritz And Other Resorts.

"No wonder smart women are so pleased"

"Naturally every woman wants to look her best . . . whether the weather man says deep snow or light rain. So I'm delighted that high fashion Hood Raintogs are back! Those wonderful Talon Boots . . . those heavenly sleek Galoshes! My how light and flexible and stretchable they are—they fit perfectly over your shoes, yet they're so easy to get on and off. And for showery weather, what could be smarter than the light, comfortable, unlined Hood Oxfords? And they come in various heel heights to fit any of your shoes. See them at your dealer's."

Footwear by
HOOD
a sure sign they're good

HOOD RUBBER COMPANY, a Division of The B. F. Goodrich Company

TEENAGER LOOKS

CASUAL:
Blue Jeans
Flannel Shirt
Moccasins
   (Replacing Saddle Shoes)

Wool jacket over blouse and skirt.

Printed crepe scarf blouse tied at waistline.

Basic blouse and full skirt cinched at waist with fabric belt and matching bolero jacket.

Clothes by Monte-Sano

Wedding-Cake Crowns

Tiered high, higher, highest for a wonderful new look.
Sharpening the excitement of the year's softer suits. Marking you
in the vanguard of a fresh fashion trend. Doubly good in
the new Stetson ceramic colors.

HORIZON GOLD... *cuff-brimmed, double-crowned for twice the smartness.* $16.95 *(Dark colors, $14.95)*
LACQUER GREEN... *a new swirled toque, sleek above your furs.* $15.95 *(Light colors, $17.95)*
CALIFORNIA BURGUNDY... *triple tiers of fine Stetson felt.* $16.95 *(Light colors, $18.95)*

STETSON HATS

AT LEADING STORES OR WRITE STETSON HATS. INC., 475 FIFTH AVENUE, NEW YORK 17, N. Y., FOR NAME OF NEAREST DEALER. ALSO MADE IN CANADA.

Miami Models Sport Newest Bonnet Fashions All Constructed From Materials Purchased From The Local Hardware Store.

A snappy little mousetrap model.

Strainers trimmed with fish scalers.

Tin plate, strainers and oil can.

A bird with ping pong balls nestled in a steel wool nest.

This miniature cannon ends the show with a big bang.

This tweed suit with classic lines is set off by a finger-length coat.

Suits once again are designed with small collars and many are belted at the waist and are finished off with embroidery trim.

Grey-beige gabardine finger-tip coat with detachable hood.

Double-breasted coat made of soft wool in a light sepia color with round shoulders and full sleeves tight at the wrist.

With restrictions lifted on many fabrics, the billowing sleeve becomes a fashion statement.

Dress necklines are either very high or provocatively low and small waistlines are emphasized.

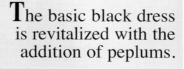

The basic black dress is revitalized with the addition of peplums.

156

SPORTS

A MILLION AND A HALF PEOPLE LINE UP TO WATCH THE 57TH ANNUAL TOURNAMENT OF ROSES PARADE IN PASADENA.

Headed by Grand Marshal Admiral Halsey, 50 flower-bedecked floats pass in review before an enthusiastic crowd.

San Francisco, United Nations Charter City, wins the prize for best depicting the theme of the pageant: Victory, Unity and Peace.

THE FAMOUS PARADE PRECEDES THE ROSE BOWL GAME.

ROSE

Later in the day, 93,000 fans jam the Rose Bowl to watch the classic struggle between Southern California and Alabama.

With Admiral Halsey looking on, Harry Gilmer picks up 12 yards for the Crimson Tide.

BOWL

34-14!

With Gilmer's long pass, the Crimson Tide whomps Southern California 34-14.

Football

■ **Two Million Ticket Requests Turned Down For Army-Navy Football Game.**

■ **National Football League Games Set New Record For Attendance With 2,671,696 Fans Turning Out.**

■ **First Major Scandal Hits Professional Football With The Discovery Of An Attempt To Bribe Two Leading Players Of The New York Football Giants To Throw The Playoff Championship Game With The Chicago Bears.**

NEW RULES IN FOOTBALL

■ **Number Of Time Outs Allotted To Each Team In Each Half Increases From Three To Four.**

■ **Larger Numbers On Uniforms Are Mandated.**

Chicago Bears Beat Giants 23-14 For NFL Title.

ARMY BEATS NAVY 21-18 IN PHILADELPHIA.

HEISMAN TROPHY WINNER:
Glenn Davis (Army)

■

COACH OF THE YEAR:
Earl "Red" Blaik (Army)

Baseball

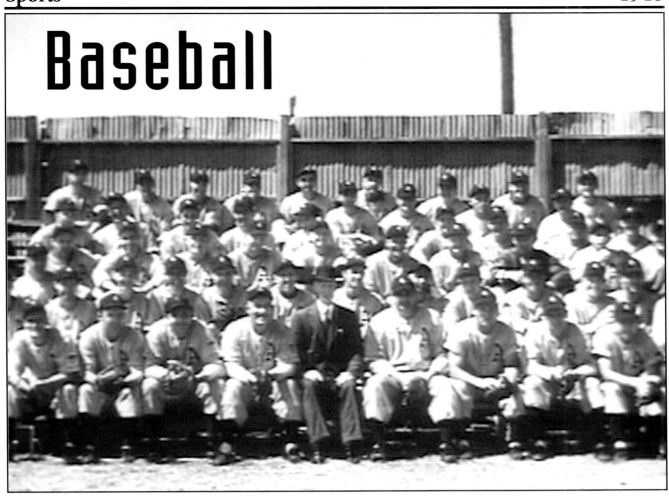

CONNIE MACK HEADS SPRING TRAINING FOR THE ATHLETICS IN WEST PALM BEACH

The pitching team lines up for practice.

Training

Dick Fowler (top, right),

Bobo Newsom (top, left) and

Russ Christopher (right) go through their paces.

Baseball's grand old man, Connie Mack, can still show the guys a thing or two.

JUNE

8 Members Of Spokane's International League Baseball Team Are Killed As Their Chartered Bus Plunges Down A 500-Foot Mountainside In The Cascades.

JULY

14 Chicago White Sox Are Kicked Out Of Game For Heckling Umpire.

AUGUST

All 8 American And National League Baseball Games Play At Night For The First Time In History.

NEW YORK YANKEES
. . . .
SIGN CONTRACT WITH UNITED AIR LINES MAKING THEM FIRST BASEBALL TEAM TO TRAVEL BY AIR FOR THE ENTIRE SEASON.

BASEBALL

 In the eighth inning of the first game of a doubleheader between the New York Giants and the Pittsburgh Pirates, Giants' manager, Mel Ott is ejected by umpire Tom Dunn. During the fifth inning of the second game, Ott protests a decision by umpire George Magerkurth and is again thumbed from the game, thus becoming the first major league manager to be thrown out of both ends of a doubleheader.

83-Year Old Connie Mack Separates From His Second Wife, Katherine.

St. Louis Defeats Boston 4-3 And Takes The World Series.

American League Wins Baseball's All-Star Game.

Shortstop JOSEPH TINKER *And 2nd Baseman* JOHN J. EVERS *Admitted To Baseball's Hall Of Fame In Cooperstown, N.Y. Along With 1st Baseman* FRANK CHANCE, *Who Died 22 Years Ago.*

MOST VALUABLE PLAYER

AMERICAN LEAGUE
Ted Williams (Boston)

NATIONAL LEAGUE
Stan Musial (St. Louis)

PASSINGS

Walter Johnson,
One Of The First 5 Members
Of Baseball's Hall Of Fame,
Dies At 59.

POCKET BILLIARDS

Jimmy Karras *(above right)* and World's Pocket Billiards Champ Willie Mosconi demonstrate special cue artistry as their cross-country match ends in Chicago.

Irving Crane Of Livonia, New York Regains World Pocket Billiards Championship.

While an appreciative audience looks on, Karras demonstrates Chinese billiards and some tricky moves.

U.S. TABLE TENNIS CHAMPIONSHIPS HELD AT ST. NICHOLAS ARENA, NEW YORK CITY

This participant demonstrates some pretty fancy footwork.

Men and women of all ages gather to compete for national table tennis honors.

DAVIS CUP Tennis Competition Resumes In Melbourne After 6 Years' Interruption Because Of The War, With The United States Team Defeating Australia 5-0.

TENNIS

U.S. LAWN TENNIS

Men's Singles
JOHN A. KRAMER
Women's Singles
PAULINE M. BETZ

WIMBLEDON

Yvon Petra
Beats
Geoff Brown

DAVIS CUP

U.S. Team Of
Jack Kramer
And Ted Schroeder
Wins Davis Cup,
Beating Australian Team.

Pauline Betz
Wins Over
Althea Brough.

GOLF

GOLFER BEN HOGAN DISCHARGED FROM THE ARMY.

BYRON NELSON LOSES UNITED STATES OPEN GOLF TITLE WHEN HIS CADDIE ACCIDENTALLY KICKS HIS BALL.

CHAMPIONS

U.S. OPEN: *Lloyd Mangrum*
PROFESSIONAL GOLFER'S ASSOCIATION: *Ben Hogan*
MASTERS TOURNAMENT: *Herman Keiser*
U.S. GOLF ASSOCIATION: *Ted Bishop*
BRITISH OPEN: *Sam Snead*

HORSE RACING

W. Mehrten Rides "Assault" To Belmont, Preakness Stakes And Kentucky Derby Win.

The National Horse Show Returns To Madison Square Garden For The First Time Since 1941.

Hans de Meiss-Teuffen Sails Solo From Spain To U.S. In 58 Days.

U.S.S.R.'s Mikhail Botvinnik Takes Over Position As World's Best Chess Player On The Death Of Aleksandr Alekhine.

John B. Kelly, Jr. (Brother Of Grace Kelly) Succeeds His Father As National Champion, Single Sculls.

BOXING

20,000 fans jam New York's Madison Square Garden for the Golden Gloves Tournament of Champions.

Ezra Gooderham, from West Virginia, (right) fights Tony Borselino from Newark, New Jersey.

■ **Tickets For Heavyweight Boxing Championship Bout Between Joe Louis And Billy Conn Soar To A Record High Of $100 Each.**

■ **Joe Louis Successfully Defends His World Heavyweight Boxing Title For the 22nd Time.**

■ **Couture Knocks Out Walton With One Punch In 10.5 Seconds Making It The Shortest Recorded Boxing Match In History.**

Gooderham K.O.'s Borselino with a mean wallop.

PASSINGS

Jack Johnson,
Former Heavyweight Champ,
Dies At 68.

SPORTS EVENTS RETURN

Fans gather to watch the first races to be held in seven years, happy to return to peaceful pursuits.

A post-war steering device is only one of the novelties in this tandem race.

TO VIENNA

The motorcycle race has the usual chills, thrills and spills.

AUTO RACING

George Robson Wins Indy 500 At 114.8 MPH.

BOWLING

Andy Varipapa Wins The All-Star Match-Game Championship In Chicago. In A 90-Day Marathon Of Bowling, Contestants Have To Throw 64 Games Across The Alleys.

HOCKEY

Montreal Beats Boston To Take The Stanley Cup.

FLICKBACK has the perfect gift to bring a nostalgic smile to the lips of anyone celebrating a birthday, anniversary or reunion. Or, why not treat yourself?

Your friend or loved one will be delighted to receive the original **FLICKBACK**, *the colorful DVD Gift Card full of stories and pictures from their fabulous year. The collector's DVD presents entertaining highlights featuring the people and events that made their year special. A dedication page conveys your personal message and an envelope is included for mailing.*

WHAT A YEAR IT WAS! *is a lavish, 176-page hardcover "scrapbook" packed with stories, photos and artwork detailing the movies, music, shows, sports, fashion, news, people, places and events that make a year unique and memorable. A special dedication page completes a truly personal yearbook gift which will be treasured for years to come.*

Explore our website or call to find a **FLICKBACK** retailer near you.

www. FLICKBACK .com

(800) 541-3533